THE DAY LINCOLN WAS SHOT

The Day LINCOLN Was Shot

AN ILLUSTRATED CHRONICLE

Richard Bak

TAYLOR PUBLISHING COMPANY, DALLAS, TEXAS

Published by Taylor Publishing Company
1550 West Mockingbird Lane
Dallas, Texas 75235

Book design by Mark McGarry
Set in Monotype Dante & Playbill

Library of Congress Cataloging-in-Publication Data
Bak, Richard, 1954–
The day Lincoln was shot : an illustrated chronicle / written by Richard Bak.
        p. cm.
    Includes bibliographical references (p. 219).
    ISBN 0–87833–200–6
        1. Lincoln, Abraham, 1809–1865 — Assassination — Pictorial works.
I. Title.
E457.5.B28   1998
973.7 ′092 — dc21   98–5311
                                                                              CIP

Printed in the United States of America
10   9   8   7   6   5   4   3   2   1

Crook, do you know I believe there are men who want to take my life? . . . I know no one could do it and escape alive. But if it is to be done, it is impossible to prevent it.

—ABRAHAM LINCOLN TO HIS BODYGUARD, APRIL 14, 1865

His name is John Wilkes Booth an actor & who has frequently played in this theater & conversant with the different places of egress from it. He had not until last night ever succeeded in attaining any reputation in his profession as an actor but now he has acquired a reputation in tragedy which will render him famous & infamous in history in all time.

—LETTER FROM EDWIN BATES TO HIS PARENTS, APRIL 15, 1865

Contents

Ford's Theater in 1865

Foreword

⊰ BY WILLIAM HANCHETT ⊱

In the chapter on the assassination of Abraham Lincoln in the fourth volume of Allan Nevins's *The War for the Union* (1971), the esteemed historian wrote: "The murder was clearly a sequel of the war, product of its senseless hatreds, fears, and cruelties. A fitting climax of the years of anger and butchery, it would help impress upon the American mind the terrible nature of the conflict."

Nevins was right that the assassination was a sequel of the war, a product of its anger and butchery. But he was incorrect about it impressing upon Americans the terrible nature of the four-year conflict. In fact, most Americans think of the assassination as completely unrelated to the war, as a freakish and artificial break in the continuity of history brought about by the madness and malevolence of assassin John Wilkes Booth. Indeed, that is how Nevins himself described Lincoln's death.

If we have failed to see how the assassination reflected the "terrible nature" of the Civil War, it is because reconciliation between North and South required that the war's fury and passion be allowed to die natural deaths. Reconciliation required a peace of good sportsmanship, the winners disdaining to gloat or take revenge, the losers being allowed to hold their heads high. The horror of a war that took the lives of some 650,000 Americans was forgotten and romance took its place.

A generation after it ended, Americans remembered a Civil War in which it would have been unthinkable for leaders of either side even to contemplate, let alone take, direct action against leaders of the other. Such has been the consensus ever since.

But readers of Richard Bak's *The Day Lincoln Was Shot*, a companion reader to the Turner Network Television film of the same name, may be surprised to find they are no longer so sure that Booth and his group acted on their own initiative. That is because the book and the film have gone to great effort to restore the assassination to its historical context. Both present a sympathetic and long-suffering Lincoln whose policies, however admirable and well intended, drove the South out of the Union and sharply divided the North, thus prolonging the war and adding immeasurably to its bitterness. Their Booth is not the one-dimensional fiend he is still widely believed to have been, but a handsome, likable, and dashing man of action completely committed to the Southern cause. Booth served the Confederacy as a spy and blockade runner and—the possibility will inevitably arise in some minds—perhaps in other ways.

Bak and TNT have borrowed their title from journalist Jim Bishop's 1955 bestseller, without doubt the most widely read of any book on the assassination. Although it made him a rich man and was translated into fourteen languages, Bishop came to regret it, for he repeated many of the discredited theories of the eccentric Chicagoan, Otto Eisenschiml, and presented a great deal of fiction as fact. As a result, millions of Americans were misinformed about a major event in their history. In his 1981 autobiography, Bishop dismissed his book as "a pile of . . . ." But readers and viewers of the new versions of *The Day Lincoln Was Shot* need have no fear; these are honest accounts of the tragedy at Ford's Theater. Bak and TNT, while obviously shaping their works to appeal to the same general audience that Bishop reached, have not sought to perpetuate old myths, but to promote an understanding of the circumstances and points of view that led to the assassination. In doing so, they advance an understanding of the "terrible nature" of the Civil War.

Unfortunately, serious study of the assassination began only recently. By the mid-twentieth century, hundreds of books and articles had been written about it, but they were mostly potboilers or reflections of the romantic tradition that described an evil madman murdering a god. The best book published before the 1980s was George S. Bryan's *The Great American Myth* (1940). Scholarly in tone, *The Great American Myth* attributed the assassination to Booth's frustration at his failure to capture Lincoln and deliver him to the Confederacy. It exposed many accumulated myths, including the one that Booth escaped and that someone else was buried in his place. But Bryan's research was confined almost exclusively to published sources. His book was thus a judicious summary of what was already known about the assassination and is likely to remain forever the classic statement of the consensus theory.

The first book on the assassination by a professional historian was not published until 1982. Thomas R. Turner's *Beware the Public Weeping: Public Opinion and the Assassination of Abraham Lincoln* corrected many misconceptions about the conspiracy trial of Booth's associates and demonstrated that the United States government had not been without grounds in charging Confederate complicity. My own *The Lincoln Murder Conspiracies* was released the following year. In researching it, I was impressed with how shallow and partisan, if not absurd, most writing on the subject had been. In 1988, *Come Retribution: The Confederate Secret Service and the Assassination of Lincoln* included far more material about Booth and the nature of his plans and actions than any previous publication. Co-authors William A. Tidwell, James O. Hall, and David Winfred Gaddy presented documentary evidence that buttressed their claim that Confederate leaders planned an attack on Lincoln, in part as retaliation for the revelation of Union plans to attack Jefferson Davis, president of the Confederacy. In Tidwell's *April '65: Confederate Covert Action in the American Civil War* (1995), the author cited additional evidence supporting the theory that, at the end of the war, Confederate leaders sought to save their sinking nation by forcibly removing Lincoln and his advisors.

Carte-de-visite *photographs of the main characters in the great national tragedy.*

Of course, not everybody agrees with Tidwell, Hall, *et al*, though the historiographic tide is turning in their direction. The literature on Lincoln, Booth, and the assassination is so vast, varied, and forever growing that it is probably impossible to find any two assassination buffs who agree on every aspect of Lincoln's murder, its motives, or the myths and minutia surrounding it. The main characters and bit actors in this great American tragedy are long gone, of course, but the ongoing public fascination about the day President Lincoln was shot guarantees that, in a larger sense, they will live on and on.

William Hanchett is a retired professor of history at San Diego State University. His many books and articles about Lincoln and the Civil War era include The Lincoln Murder Conspiracies *and* Irish: Charles G. Halpine in Civil War America.

A Confederate soldier killed at Spotsylvania in the bloody spring of 1864.

This Dreadful War

FOUR YEARS. HAD IT REALLY BEEN THAT LONG?
As Abraham Lincoln prepared remarks for his second inaugural speech, he
hoped to deliver a message that would help a torn, bleeding country to
look with guarded optimism and unshakable faith towards a better future—one
free of mutually destructive feuds and rivalries. But such an address necessarily
entailed perspective: looking back on four years of what the president had come
to call "this dreadful war." "When I think of the sacrifice yet to be offered and
the hearts and homes yet to be made desolate before this dreadful war is over,"
he had confessed in a troubled moment, "my heart is like lead within me, and I
feel at times like hiding in a deep darkness."

Lately the whirlwind seemed to have taken on hurricane-force proportions.
Much of the South lay in ruins, whole cities and isolated farms gutted by the
scythe-like advances of General Sherman's "bummers." The Confederate capital of Richmond was slowly being strangled by General Grant's army; soon it,
too, would be in flames. The death toll on all fronts was steadily approaching its
final figure of some 650,000 on both sides—a staggering figure, roughly equal to
those killed in all of America's previous and future wars combined. The number of combatants and civilians permanently crippled in either body or mind by
their experiences was anybody's guess.

Sorrow had seeped into the White House. The war was only a few weeks old
when a close family friend, a young colonel named Elmer Ellsworth, was shot

dead by an innkeeper while tearing down a rebel flag in Alexandria, Virginia. The senselessness of it saddened the president, who henceforth struggled to depersonalize the casualty

The effects of four wartime years in the White House can be seen in these comparative photographs of Lincoln. At left is how he appeared on June 3, 1860, shortly after being nominated for the presidency. At right is how he looked on Palm Sunday, 1865, the day General Robert E. Lee surrendered at Appomattox.

reports he read every night in the telegraph office of the War Department. Mary Lincoln, the First Lady, had several members of her extended family fight and fall, all in the cause of the Confederacy. Samuel Todd was killed at Shiloh in 1862; the following year two more half-brothers, Captain David H. Todd and Alexander H. Todd, died at Vicksburg and Baton Rouge, respectively. That same year her half-sister's husband, General Ben Hardin Helm, was killed at Chickamauga.

The Lincolns had two sons in uniform, in a fashion. Young Thomas—nicknamed "Tad" for "Tadpole"—playfully strutted around the executive mansion in a colonel's uniform cut down to size. Twenty-one-year-old Robert, a Harvard graduate who had finally wrangled a captain's commission over the objections of his worried mother, served on Grant's staff. But there was a tremendous void in the household. In 1862, eleven-year-old Willie's death from fever had plunged his parents into deep gloom, one that was still apparent to Vinnie Ream three years later as she attempted to sculpt the president's likeness. Ream remembered Lincoln "slouched into a chair at his desk, his huge feet extended and his head bowed on his chest, deeply thoughtful." At these times she imagined him "hearing the cries of suffering that were coming from the prisons and the sobs for sons, lost like his own. . . . Never was there grief equal to Lincoln's."

Unlike Lincoln's first inauguration, which had taken place on a clear, sunny day, a drizzle fell on the morning of March 4, 1865. The effects of worry and fatigue were clearly visible in Lincoln's lined, rumpled face as he rose to make his second inaugural address on a platform in front of the Capitol dome.

Several hundred feet away was photographer Alexander Gardner, once an assistant to the famous Mathew Brady. Over the years Gardner had taken many of the photographs of battlefield dead attributed to Brady, rearranging their shattered limbs and broken muskets for dramatic effect while being careful not to offend the buying public by being *too* realistic. Now, on this raw, wet Saturday, Gardner took several long exposures as the president summarized the underlying causes of the conflict before expressing his magnanimity towards the soon-to-be-vanquished South.

"With malice toward none," he concluded, "with charity for all; with firmness in the right, as God gives us to see the right, let us strive on to finish the work we are in; to bind up the nation's wounds; to care for him who shall have borne the battle, and for his widow, and his orphan—to do all which may achieve and cherish a just, and a lasting peace, among ourselves, and with all nations."

The president kissed the Bible. Just then, as if a higher authority was managing stage directions, the sun broke through, casting a welcome warmth over the faces of those in the damp crowd.

One of those faces belonged to a dapper young actor named John Wilkes Booth, who can be spotted in the far right hand corner of one of Gardner's photographs. He is standing no more than fifty feet away from the little white table at which Lincoln spoke. It is remarkable, really, given future events, that two men destined to be forever linked in history and folklore would be photographed so close together. While the president spoke eloquently of mercy and rapprochement, Booth had entertained more sinister thoughts. "What an excellent chance I had to kill the president," he later told an actor friend, "if I had wished, on Inauguration Day!"

Although they never met, the president and his future assassin had crossed paths before, and would again one final, fateful evening six weeks later. However, up to the very last moments

Lincoln's rebel brothers-in-law. From left: Captain David H. Todd, Alexander Todd, and General Ben Hardin Helm.

of his life Lincoln would know Booth only as an accomplished actor whose performances he had occasionally enjoyed over the years, and not as the misguided Southern patriot whose derringer blast sent him prematurely to eternity.

There was, for example, Lincoln's arrival in Albany in 1861, as the president-elect made his way by train to Washington City (as Washington, D.C., was then called). Booth, then appearing at the Gayety Theater, was so outspokenly secessionist in his views that hotel management threatened to kick him out. "Is this not a Democratic city?" argued Booth. "Democratic, yes," was the response. "But disunion—no!"

Two years later, Lincoln and his wife—both regular theatergoers—were in attendance as Booth performed for the first time in New York City. On a subsequent occasion, Lincoln marveled over the energetic actor's performance in *The Marble Heart*. Informed of the president's favorable review of his work, Booth was anything but flattered.

The earliest known portrait of Lincoln is this daguerreotype taken by N.H. Shepherd in Springfield, Illinois, in 1846. That year Lincoln was elected to Congress.

"I would rather have the applause of a nigger," he sneered. As events would reveal, what Booth really sought was the acclaim of a far larger audience—the grateful South.

★

Abraham Lincoln was born on February 12, 1809, inside a drafty, sparsely furnished log cabin located near present-day

Hodgenville, Kentucky. Lincoln's mother had been an illegitimate child and his father was an illiterate with no appreciation for book learning, facts that shamed Lincoln as much as the grinding poverty in which he grew up. For these reasons he rarely spoke of his early years, even as the myths surrounding his log-cabin origins seized the public imagination later in life. He distanced himself from his father, refusing to invite him to his wedding in 1842 and failing to attend his funeral a few years later.

Books rarely were part of a young boy's rough-and-tumble upbringing on the frontier. "There were some schools, so called," he remembered, "but no qualification was ever required of a teacher beyond readin', writin', and cipherin' to the rule of three. If a straggler supposed to understand Latin happened to sojourn in the neighborhood, he was looked upon as a wizard. There was absolutely nothing to excite ambition for education."

Despite these obstacles, Lincoln managed to accumulate an education by "littles," as he described it—a little now and a little then. His entire formal schooling amounted to less than a year. His main inspiration was his stepmother, Sarah Bush Johnston, who entered his life when he was nine, shortly after his mother had died from drinking tainted cow's milk. She encouraged her lanky, tousled-hair stepson and provided a loving environment inside the smoky, crowded cabin.

By now the family was living in Perry County, Indiana, a state that had just entered the Union. The long-limbed boy worked the farm and contributed to the family income through such odd jobs as splitting wood and operating a ferry. When he was nineteen he accompanied a local merchant on a twelve-hundred-mile flatboat journey down the Ohio and Mississippi Rivers to New Orleans. The three-month trip netted Lincoln twenty-four dollars. It also opened his eyes to opportunities outside his immediate backwoods world.

In 1830, the family moved again, this time to a site in central Illinois, near Decatur. After helping his father build a cabin, Lincoln took another flatboat of cargo to New Orleans. When he returned, he said farewell to farm life and moved to New Salem—a "friendless, uneducated, penniless boy" of twenty-two, he later recalled. He clerked at a general store and slept in

Mary Todd Lincoln in 1846.

the back room. Self-conscious about his lack of education, but eager to move in higher circles, Lincoln joined the local debating society. He borrowed books from a fellow debater and proved himself a capable speaker. "All he lacked was culture," recalled one neighbor.

After the store closed, he also lacked a job. Having developed a keen interest in law and politics through his reading and debating, he decided to run for the Illinois state legislature. To further his chances, he volunteered for a militia company being formed to fight Chief Black Hawk of the warring Sauk and Fox tribes. His fellow volunteers elected him captain, but his tour was short and uneventful and failed to impress voters. He finished eighth among thirteen candidates. But friends soon secured for him the part-time position of postmaster of New Salem. Coupled with his duties in his new job as a deputy surveyor, his name soon became known around the county. In 1834, he ran for the state legislature again. This time he was elected. It was the start of a long political career that would span thirty-one years and eventually place him in the White House.

Lincoln served in the Illinois legislature from 1834 to 1841. In 1836, he was admitted to the state bar and moved to the capital of Springfield. There he began a very successful law practice and also started a family. On November 4, 1842, he married twenty-six-year-old Mary Todd, the spoiled and mercurial daughter of a rich Kentucky banker. The following August she gave birth to Robert Todd Lincoln, the first of four boys and the only one to live past eighteen.

Mary, or "Mother" as Lincoln lovingly called her, was plagued by migraine headaches and susceptible to irrational fits of rage. She once chased her husband out of their Springfield home with a butcher knife. "Whenever Mrs. L got the devil in her," recalled a neighbor, "Lincoln would pick up

One of the men Lincoln most admired was Daniel Webster. The legendary political figure stirred Lincoln with his oration, particularly his famous "Reply to Hayne," a speech that closed with the invocation: "Liberty and Union, now and forever, one and inseparable!" As a young congressman, Lincoln freely borrowed from Webster's speeches and sought his company. He may also have been influenced by the great man's choice of headgear: a stovepipe hat.

one of his children and walk off—would laugh at her—pay no earthly attention to her when in that wild furious condition."

The biggest point of contention between the two was the amount of time Lincoln spent away from home pursuing his passion of politics. He had become a popular speaker and important organizer, emerging as the Whig floor leader during his four terms in the state legislature. His reward was the Whig nomination for Congress in 1846. As congressman, Lincoln was his own man, presenting a bill that sought to abolish slavery in the District of Columbia and taking an unpopular stand against the "immoral and unnecessary" Mexican War of 1846–1848. His views, however, left him empty-handed when plum political appointments were handed out. Disappointed by the reaction of party leaders, he returned to the full-time practice of law and, in 1854, to the Illinois legislature. After an unsuccessful bid for a Senate seat in 1855, he switched to the more progressive Republican Party.

The Lincoln of this period was an imposing physical specimen. He stood six feet, four inches high, a good eight inches taller than the average adult male. His strength was prodigious. "If you heard him fellin' trees in a clearin' you would say there was three men at work by the way the trees fell," said his cousin, Dennis Hanks. Even in the final year of his life, he could grab a heavy axe by the end of its handle and hold it straight out from his shoulder.

He also was homely—the main reason, perhaps, that he didn't marry until he was thirty-three years old. One observer referred to his face as being "ploughed." Unfortunately, pictures of the man emphasize his homeliness at the expense of his humanity. The technology of photography in those days required the subject to sit still for several minutes as the picture developed; any movement would cause a blurred image. The impression future generations were left with is that nobody in the middle nineteenth century ever smiled. In reality, the solemn, stone-faced images of Lincoln that we have come to know from history books, pennies, five-dollar bills, and Mount Rushmore are completely at odds with the Lincoln whose everyday choice was to laugh as long, hard, and often as possible. He often told the same joke, anecdote, or tall tale several times in one day. In these moments of mirth, his features came

Eleven-year-old Willie Lincoln died in 1862, plunging his mother into grief and his father into melancholy. "It is hard, hard to have him die," said Lincoln. Three years later Willie's body would join his father's on the funeral train back to Illinois.

alive, said his law partner, William Herndon: "His little gray eyes sparkled; a smile seemed to gather up, curtain like, the corners of his mouth; his frame quivered with suppressed excitement; and, when the point—or 'nub' of the story, as he called it—came, no one's laugh was heartier than his."

Abolitionist John Brown, pictured here in a mural by John Steuart Curry, was considered a martyr in the North but viewed as a wild-eyed Satan in the South. One of the people present at his execution on December 2, 1859, was John Wilkes Booth, who became sick at the sight of the hanging.

His humor could be sophisticated or bawdy, depending on the audience. In a men's-only environment he might trot out the old favorite about a well-endowed slave whose phallus was used as a razor strop, or the tale about the self-possessed dinner guest who farted after being invited to carve the turkey. His humor on the campaign trail often was self-deprecating. He

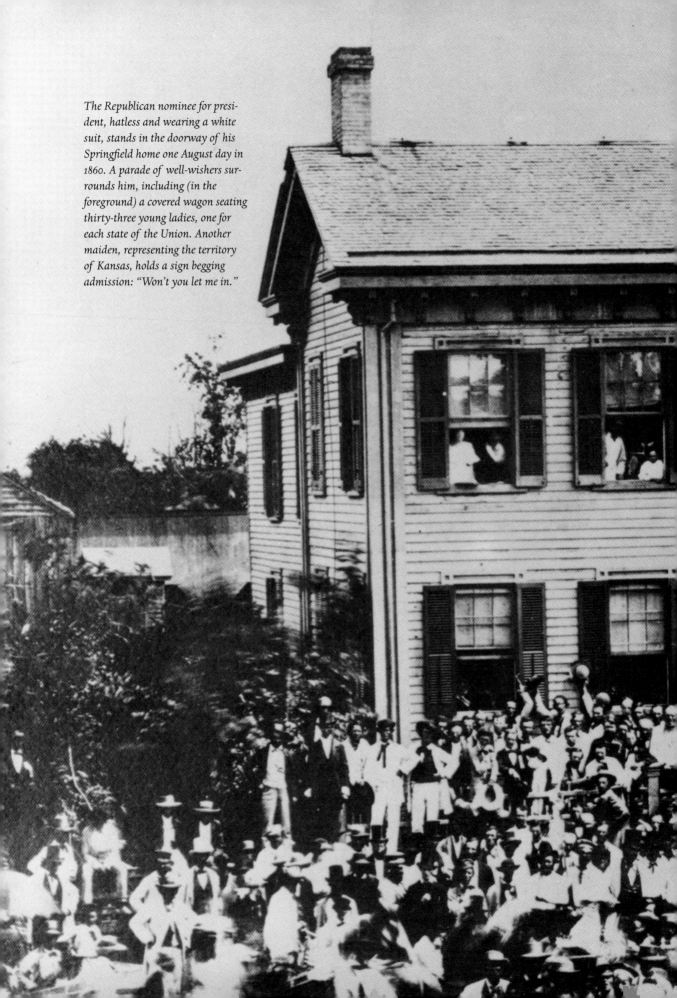

The Republican nominee for president, hatless and wearing a white suit, stands in the doorway of his Springfield home one August day in 1860. A parade of well-wishers surrounds him, including (in the foreground) a covered wagon seating thirty-three young ladies, one for each state of the Union. Another maiden, representing the territory of Kansas, holds a sign begging admission: "Won't you let me in."

enjoyed telling of the stranger who pulled a knife out of his pocket. Handing it to Lincoln, the stranger explained that it had been given to him with the order "that I was to keep it until I found a man uglier than myself. Allow me now to say, sir, that I think *you* are fairly entitled to the property."

"Some of the stories are not so nice as they might be," Lincoln admitted, "but I tell you the truth when I say that a funny story, if it has the element of genuine wit, has the same effect on me that I suppose a good square drink of whiskey has on an old toper; it puts new life into me."

He needed the release, for violent, sudden death was a staple of the frontier and remained a recurring theme of his life. His paternal grandfather and namesake had been killed by an Indian while working in the fields on his Kentucky farm. By his eighteenth year he had watched his mother and baby brother succumb to disease and his older sister die in childbirth. In 1850, his second son, Eddy, died of tuberculosis just before his fourth birthday. Another young son, Willie, died in 1862.

As a middle-aged man, Lincoln once revisited the scenes of his Indiana boyhood. The experience moved him to verse:

> *My childhood's home I see again*
> *And sadden with the view;*
> *And still, as memory crowds my brain,*
> *There's pleasure in it too.*
> *O Memory! Thou midway world*
> *Twixt earth and paradise,*
> *Where things decayed and loved ones lost*
> *In dreamy shadows rise,*
> *And, freed from all that's earthly vile,*
> *Seem hallowed, pure, and bright,*
> *Like scenes in some enchanted isle*
> *All bathed in liquid light.*

The lines not only hinted at Lincoln's literary ability, which was considerable, but reflected the author's melancholy, which grew deeper with age. Steeled and saddened by his experiences with early death, he struggled to reconcile his ambitiousness with regular musings about mortality and predetermination. In these dark, introspective moments he supposed all events to be

Publisher Frank Leslie summarized the president-elect's life story in his weekly illustrated newspaper.

Lincoln was inaugurated on March 4, 1861, the first of his 1,504 days in the White House.

"Wide-Awakes" march through the streets of New York, drumming up support for their candidate. Lincoln won the 1860 presidential election, but with just forty per-cent of the popular vote. "Well, boys," he told a group of friends, "your troubles are over now, but mine have just begun."

The Confederate flag flies over Fort Sumter.

fixed in advance, beyond the capacity of ordinary human beings to influence. Even the greatest man was little more than a twig floating down the mighty Mississippi of time.

"I have all my life been a fatalist," he admitted as president. "What is to be will be, or rather, I have found all my life as Hamlet says, 'There is a divinity that shapes our ends, Rough hew them how we will.'"

★

Lincoln considered himself a modern and forward-thinking man. In 1836, he became the first major American political leader to publicly advocate women's suffrage. In 1849, he invented a device (U.S. Patent No. 6,469) for lifting boats over shoals by means of "buoyant air chambers." It was his views on the issue of slavery, however, that fueled his political comeback and elevated him to national prominence on the eve of the Civil War.

In 1854, the controversial Kansas-Nebraska Act was pushed through Congress by Stephen A. Douglas, the diminutive sena-tor from Illinois. The legislation, in effect, permitted slavery in newly opened territories. The country already was split into opposing camps: Northern states opposed slavery while Southern states favored it. Now, new states in the process of drafting constitutions were being asked to choose for themselves, a situa-tion that had fanatics from both sides of the slavery question issuing speeches and threats in order to influence the decision.

The most infamous of these agitators was John Brown, a wild-eyed, bushy-bearded aboli-tionist who led his guerrilla band in a divine call to action against pro-slavery factions. In 1856 Brown's men murdered five settlers near Pottawatomie, Kansas. His hanging three years later after leading an attack on the federal arse-nal in Harper's Ferry, Virginia, would make him a martyr in the North.

During the 1858 race for the U.S. Senate, anti-slavery Republicans backed Lincoln in his bid to upset Douglas, the Democratic incumbent. Douglas agreed to a series of seven public debates around the state that clarified each can-didate's stand. Large crowds attended each meeting: 15,000 in Freeport and more than 12,000 in Ottawa and Charleston. Douglas, a gifted orator, declared that "this government can exist . . . divided into free and slave states." Lincoln, like Douglas, did not believe in black equality. But he passionately believed in free-dom for all people, regardless of skin color. He called slavery a moral and a social wrong.

"The Little Giant," Stephen Douglas, was born in Vermont and was an apprentice cabinetmaker before heading west and taking up law. In 1858 the diminutive Democratic senator from Illinois engaged Lincoln in a series of debates that made his towering opponent a national figure. Having seen his party and the country divide over the issues of slavery and states' rights, Douglas would not live to see the outcome of the war. He died June 3, 1861, in Chicago of typhoid fever.

Douglas won the election, but Lincoln became a national figure through his spirited and rational attack on slavery. He

$200 REWARD.

I will give the above reward for the apprehension of Ludwell, if taken in the state of Pennsylvania or any other Northern State and secured so that he is delivered to me or my agent; or $150 if taken in the State of Maryland or the District of Columbia. Ludwell ran away from Waverly, near the Warrenton Springs, on the 21st of October; he is 18 or 19 years old, dark complexion, about 5½ feet high, and walks rather awkwardly and sluggishly. Had on when he left a dark colored sack coat, light pantaloons, a dark cloth cap and boots. He left in company with a slave of Mr. Parr's, of Culpeper County, who, I understand, is of low statue and black.

JOHN W. TYLER,
Warrenton, Fauquier Co., Va.
Oct. 28, 1854.

An 1854 poster offering a reward for a runaway slave.

also caused a major rift in the Democratic Party by forcing Douglas into making a statement that slavery could be excluded from a new territory before a state constitution was drafted. Two years later, when it came time to select a candidate for president, antagonized Southern Democrats refused to endorse the Northern Democrats' nomination of Douglas. They decided to back their own man, former vice president John C. Breckinridge of Kentucky.

Meanwhile, Lincoln was nominated on the third ballot at the Republican national convention in Chicago. He clearly was a compromise choice, not only of his party, but of the nation. By nightfall on November 6, 1860, fireworks and torchlight parades lit up Springfield. The final tally showed Lincoln receiving 1,866,000 votes to 1,377,000 for Douglas and 850,000 for Breckinridge. Although he had gathered only forty percent of the popular vote and his name hadn't even appeared on Southern ballots, the fifty-one-year-old Lincoln would succeed James Buchanan as president.

★

"Today was inaugurated that wretch, Abraham Lincoln, President of the U.S.," Catherine Deveraux Edmondston, the matriarch of a North Carolina plantation, wrote in her diary on March 4, 1861, the day Lincoln took the oath of office. "We are told not to speak evil of dignities—but it is hard to realize that he is a dignity. Ah, would that Jefferson Davis were our President. He is a man to whom a gentleman could look, without mortification, as chief of the nation. Well—we have a rail-splitter and a tall man at the head of our affairs!"

Between the time of Lincoln's election and his inauguration, the long, slow slide toward civil war was completed. With one in four Southerners owning slaves and the economy of the whole region dependent on forced labor, the major dispute remained clear and insoluble. But the industrial North and agrarian South also disagreed over such issues as tariffs and the power of the federal government. The lack of compromise made a split along regional lines inevitable.

Claiming it had no other recourse, on December 20, 1860, South Carolina announced that it was seceding from the Union. Three weeks later, on January 9, 1861, its militia fired on

A family of slaves picks cotton. Lincoln did not believe in the equality of races, but he did consider slavery to be morally wrong. Upon the advice of others, he waited until it was politically expedient—after a Union victory at Antietam on September 22, 1862—before issuing his Emancipation Proclamation.

a steamer delivering supplies to the federal troops hunkered inside Fort Sumter, off the coast of Charleston. These were the first shots of the Civil War. That same day Mississippi seceded, followed by Florida, Alabama, Georgia, Louisiana, and Texas. On February 4, the seven states met to form the Confederate States of America. Jefferson Davis, a Mississippi senator who had been secretary of war under Franklin Pierce, was inaugurated as president of the new nation, which by the end of May had grown to include Virginia, Arkansas, Tennessee, and North Carolina.

The Battle of Bull Run, fought at Manassas, Virginia, in July 1861, was the first major clash of the war and a devastating blow to those Northerners who envisioned a quick end to the rebellion.

To the incoming president, the Confederacy was an outlaw nation. Lincoln's single objective was to bring these eleven states back into the fold. Abolishing slavery was secondary; preserving the Union was paramount. With Congress in recess, he assumed broad executive powers. He called for a blockade of Southern ports, suspended the right of habeas corpus (which forbids imprisonment without trial), and, upon the fall of Fort Sumter on April 14, asked states to provide him with 75,000 troops for ninety days in order to put down the rebellion.

Lincoln was overly optimistic. Although the Confederacy had a population of only 9 million (4 million of them slaves) compared to the Union's 22 million, and lacked the North's industrial capabilities, it fielded fine armies under competent commanders. Moreover, as much of the fighting occurred in Confederate territory, they fought with the bulldog tenacity of people defending their home turf.

A glimpse of what was to come occurred on Sunday, July 21, 1861, when the Rebels routed green Union troops near the rail junction of Manassas, Virginia. Soldiers threw down rifles and joined newspapermen, politicians, and picnickers in fleeing the

Thomas Lincoln, Jr., nicknamed "Tad" for "Tadpole," with his father in 1865.

The Lincolns' oldest son, Robert. Born in 1843, he attended Harvard before serving as an officer in the war. He would be the only one of four boys to live past eighteen.

countryside for the safety of Washington. Bull Run, as the battle was called in the North, dashed hopes of a quick victory. It also was the start of Lincoln's concerns over the way professional soldiers conducted war. He grew dissatisfied with the caution and indecision of generals like George B. McClellan and Henry Halleck and reluctantly took a more active role as commander in chief. It wasn't until early 1864, when Ulysses S. Grant was made the new general in chief of all Union armies, that Lincoln finally found the man who could wage war terribly and stubbornly enough to win.

By then the fighting had lasted three years, with casualty figures climbing and no real end in sight. Public opinion had swung against the war in the North. There had been an ugly riot in New York City when Lincoln instituted the first nationwide draft in 1863, and noisy "Peace Democrats"—dubbed "Copperheads"—were declaring the war a failure and calling for its immediate end. However, though it wasn't readily clear

Lincoln stands hatless in the center in the only known photograph of him at Gettysburg. The speech he is preparing to deliver will be so short—barely two minutes—that photographers will have no time to set up their cameras for a better shot.

at the time, the corner had been turned, thanks to an astute political move by Lincoln and the sacrifice of thousands of men at the costliest battle in American history.

On September 22, 1862, Lincoln issued his preliminary Emancipation Proclamation, which freed the slaves, effective January 1, 1863. The president had shrewdly waited to release his controversial proclamation until after a big Union victory at Antietam, Maryland, then—unwilling to upset loyal slaveholding border states like Kentucky and Missouri—hedged his bets by specifying that it referred only to those slaves held in Confederate territory. The declaration of emancipation helped win crucial European support for the Union, broadened war aims by making the conflict a struggle for human freedom, and provided the depleted Union ranks with tens of thousands of fresh Negro troops, all eager to demonstrate their race's adulation of "Father Abraham."

Privately, Lincoln thought his proclamation of emancipation, issued under the vaguely defined "war powers," was probably unconstitutional. Publicly, he chastised those Northerners who howled over the idea of millions of liberated slaves: "You say you will not fight to free Negroes. Some of them seem willing to fight for you. . . . Why should they do anything for us, if we will do nothing for them? If they stake their lives for us, they must be prompted by the strongest motive—even the promise of freedom. And the promise being made, must be kept."

John Lincoln Clem of the 22nd Michigan was only ten years old when he won fame as the "Drummer Boy of Chickamauga" for shooting a Confederate officer off his horse. Thousands of similarly high-spirited, patriotic youths served in Mr. Lincoln's army, a situation that distressed the commander in chief. He regularly remitted the death sentences of youngsters caught napping on guard duty, once commenting that the guilty party deserved to be sent home to his mother and spanked, not shot.

★

Time and nature have had their way with the scarred countryside surrounding Gettysburg, 135 years after chance selected the sleepy Pennsylvania town as the site of the decisive battle of the Civil War. Today, the pockmarked ridges and fields are smoothed over, the final resting places of thousands of soldiers all overgrown by the lush grass that poet Walt Whitman called "the beautiful uncut hair of graves." Every year more than a million people visit America's most famous battlefield. Children chatter and treat the meadows as a playground. Adults exhibit a keener sense of history. They stand solemn as owls next to cannons and in front of markers, heads slightly

This Currier & Ives cartoon from the 1864 presidential campaign shows General McClellan, the Democrats' "peace candidate," trying to prevent Lincoln and Jefferson Davis from tearing the Union apart.

cocked as if to recapture the sound of a distant drumroll or a whiff of ancient gunsmoke.

Although the fury of those first three days in July 1863 has long since been spent, the battlefield continues its hold on the imagination. What if General Robert E. Lee and his Army of Northern Virginia had been victorious at Gettysburg?

Most probably the South would have been in a position to win a political, if not military, victory over the North, and the United States today would share a common border with a sovereign nation known as the Confederate States of America. Surely much of the flow of world history would have been disrupted by the social, political, and economic splintering of one great nation into two.

Such conjecture was made moot at Gettysburg, where for three muggy days a Confederate force of 75,000 men hurled itself at 90,000 Yankees. After General George Pickett's story-

book charge across an open field and up the slopes of
Cemetery Ridge ended in a spectacular failure, Lee's beaten
army withdrew to Virginia, the upstart South's fate more or
less sealed. Heavy thunderstorms soaked the twenty-five-
square-mile battlefield, which was left littered with the
canteens, rifles, letters, combs, knapsacks, daguerreotypes,
and bloated bodies of more than 40,000 dead and wounded
men.

On November 19, 1863, Lincoln traveled to Gettysburg to
dedicate the seventeen acres of land that had been set aside as
a cemetery for the Union and Confederate dead. After the
noted scholar Edward Everett spoke for two hours, the president rose to read some brief remarks. "Fourscore and seven
years ago," he began in his reedy voice, "our fathers brought
forth on this continent a new nation, conceived in liberty and
dedicated to the proposition that all men are created equal.

"Now we are engaged in a great civil war, testing whether
that nation—or any nation, so conceived and so dedicated—can
long endure. We are met on a great battlefield of that war. We
have come to dedicate a portion of that field as the final resting
place for those who here gave their lives that that nation might
live. It is altogether fitting and proper that we should do this.

"But in a larger sense, we cannot dedicate, we cannot conse-
crate, we cannot hallow this ground. The brave men, living
and dead, who struggled here, have consecrated it, far above
our power to add or to detract. The world will very little note
nor long remember what we say here; but it can never forget
what they did here. It is for us, the living, rather, to be dedicated, here, to the unfinished work that they have thus far so
nobly carried on. It is rather for us to be here dedicated to the
great task remaining before us; that from these honored dead
we take increased devotion to that cause for which they gave
the last full measure of devotion; that we here highly resolve
that these dead shall not have died in vain; that this nation,
under God, shall have a new birth of freedom, and that government of the people, by the people, for the people, shall not
perish from the earth."

The two-minute speech was so brief that photographers
failed to get a shot of Lincoln delivering it. Which to the president was just as well, since he didn't think much of its quality

Although he was not eligible for the draft, Lincoln decided upon the symbolic act of sending a representative in his place. In 1864, just weeks before the presidential election, he paid John Summerfield Staples $500 to bear his musket. The twenty-year-old carpenter from Stroudsburg, Pennsylvania, was a full ten inches shorter than the president, prompting a sergeant to ask upon his reporting for duty with the 2nd District of Columbia Volunteers: "Aren't you just the first installment?" This was Staples' second stint as a substitute; in an earlier tour with the 176th Pennsylvania he had survived combat in North Carolina and a bout with typhoid fever. Like Lincoln, Staples would die suddenly in a rocking chair—of a heart attack, at age forty-three, inside a boarding-house in Dover, New Jersey.

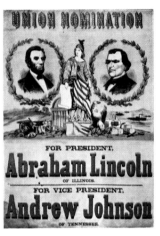

Thanks in part to the overwhelming support of his soldiers, many of whom were granted furloughs to vote, Lincoln defeated McClellan in the 1864 election. As much as anything, his re-election meant the Union would ultimately prevail in what had become a war of attrition.

or impact. History has been kinder. Powerful in its utter simplicity, the Gettysburg Address lives on as the most famous piece of oratory to come out of the war.

★

Lincoln heartily disliked being called Abe, but he had no quarrel with the 8th Wisconsin choosing to name its eagle mascot "Old Abe" after him. Confederates made the handsome bird with the six-and-a-half-foot wingspan the target of bullets and such derisive nicknames as "Turkey Buzzard," but Old Abe survived three years of action and was retired to a room in the basement of the state capitol in Madison.

The Emancipation Proclamation and the Gettysburg Address are two of Lincoln's greatest legacies, but it was the bloody business of waging total war that occupied his thoughts in the summer of 1864, as General Grant launched an all-out offensive on Richmond. Fifty-four thousand Yankees fell and still the capital of the Confederacy remained in rebel control. Lincoln found it difficult to stomach the slaughter, particularly with an election looming, but he stood by his commander. Although both were loathe to admit it publicly, they understood that the North would ultimately win a war of attrition—assuming Lincoln was able to stay in office.

He had the support of Republicans and "war Democrats" and was nominated for a second term. His opponent in the 1864 presidential election was none other than General George McClellan, a "peace candidate" who vowed to end the war and restore slavery. His promises sounded good to Northerners worn out by the unceasing sacrifice of men and money. But as election day neared, electrifying news came from the front.

General William T. Sherman had taken Atlanta and started a devastating sweep through Georgia. Meanwhile, General Phil Sheridan's cavalry was slashing its way through the Shenandoah Valley and Grant continued to pound away at the defenses around Richmond.

For the first time since Lincoln took office four years earlier, the war without end now seemed to have one. On November 8, 1864, voters kept him in the White House by a margin of nearly a half-million votes.

With re-election came a fresh flurry of assassination threats, which Lincoln filed in a pigeonhole of his desk. Truth be told, it was a simple matter to kill a high public official, even the president of the United States, and he knew it.

"Long Abraham Lincoln a Little Longer." This caricature, published in Harper's Weekly *the day before the 1864 election, proved unintentionally prescient. At the time the president had less than five and a half months to live.*

The Changing Wartime Image of Lincoln

⊰ BY HAROLD HOLZER ⊱

"OF ALL THE MEN about Washington," the *Chicago Tribune* proclaimed during one of the Union's darkest hours of the Civil War, "Abraham Lincoln is the best fitted to take command of the army."

To the influential newspaper, the evidence supporting this bold statement was abundant. Lincoln understood more about strategy than any of his advisors, "civil or military." He even knew the terrain—"every path, road, defile, mountain, stream, and wood," claimed the paper's editors. As "president, general in chief, and secretary of war in one," the *Tribune* confidently predicted, he would surely "lead our armies to victory. We sincerely believe he can do it."

By the time the *Tribune* issued its recommendation, however, Northern civilians had, for three long years, seen Lincoln depicted in ways strongly suggesting that he was the quintessential civilian, not a military man. Consequently, even after formally trained commanders like Irvin McDowell, John Pope, Ambrose Burnside, and Joseph Hooker had failed miserably on the battlefield, few Northerners were ready to believe in Lincoln's ability to lead troops.

Actually, Lincoln probably would have welcomed the opportunity to take to the field of battle. In 1832, while he was still a young man living in the frontier village of New Salem, Illinois, war had broken out with the Fox and Sac (Sauk) Indians led by Chief Black Hawk. When Lincoln enlisted in the local militia, his fellow volunteers, to his "surprize," elected him their captain. No success, he later admitted, ever gave him "so much satisfaction." But Lincoln harbored no illusions about his war service.

"[D]id you know I am a military hero?" he joked from the floor of Congress in 1848. "Yes sir; in the days of the Black Hawk War, I fought, bled, and came away." He never saw any Indians, he confessed, "but I had a good many bloody struggles"—with mosquitos.

Lincoln worried profoundly about the hypnotic allure of military glory, "that attractive rainbow that rises in showers of blood—that serpent's eye that charms to destroy." He opposed the Mexican War of 1846–48, a stand

Early Lincoln prints often emphasized his frontier origins, depicting him chopping wood, splitting rails, or guiding a flatboat.

that for years thwarted his political aspirations. And when Lincoln challenged Democrat Stephen A. Douglas for his Senate seat in 1858, his rival did not hesitate to remind voters that Lincoln had taken "the side of the common enemy, in time of war, against his own country."

Lincoln lost the Senate race, but two years later he won the Republican nomination for president. Americans, curious about this virtually unknown candidate, clamored for portraits of Lincoln that would serve as an introduction and provide biographical information. Printmakers responded with images that stressed Lincoln's attributes—most of which were physical, though decidedly civilian. Portrayed as a woodchopper, railsplitter, and flatboatman, Lincoln became the epitome of the American success story, one who had escaped frontier poverty through sweat and strength.

Unfortunately for Lincoln, his public image was dealt a severe blow in February 1861 by the events surrounding his journey as president-elect from Springfield, Illinois, to Washington, D.C., for his March 4 inauguration. Warned of assassination plots brewing in Baltimore—a necessary stop en route and a haven for anti-Lincoln sentiment—he submitted to the protection of the Pinkerton Detective Agency, whose agents, having prevailed upon him to disguise himself in an uncharacteristic soft hat and an overcoat, rushed him through the city by night on a special train. Learning of the Baltimore incident, Northern artists bombarded the weekly periodicals with cartoons of Lincoln fleeing the city in fear, wickedly exaggerating his disguise as a comical Scotch cap and a military cape. Never had a president assumed office with so negative a persona.

Civil War scholar T. Harry Williams claimed that Lincoln not only rebounded from this inauspicious start, but also grew into a better strategist "than any of his generals," becoming "in actuality as well as in title the commander in chief." More recently, Lincoln biographer David Herbert Donald described the president's rapid development from an "inexperienced" and "overworked" administrator to a chief executive who was firmly in charge.

At the beginning of the war, Unionists must have been disheartened by the comparisons between Lincoln and his wholly military counterpart, the Confederacy's President Jefferson Davis. Like Lincoln, Davis had fought in the Black Hawk War, but there the two men's military resumes sharply diverged. Davis had gone on to graduate from West Point and win glory in the Mexican War that Lincoln had spoken out against.

Printmakers capitalized immediately on the differences between the two presidents. A New York lithographer issued a print entitled *Jefferson Davis and his Generals* that showed the Confederate commander in chief, in full military dress, with Generals Robert E. Lee, Joseph E. Johnston, Thomas J. "Stonewall" Jackson, and others. A Richmond lithographer, inspired by false rumors that Davis had led troops during the 1861 Southern victory at Bull Run, issued a best-selling portrait of the Confederate president on horseback, conferring with his officers on the battlefield.

Lincoln could not hope to compete with such martial imagery, however exaggerated. There were parlor prints depicting him in early councils of war with his generals, but such renderings could not promote the notion that Lincoln, in his familiar swallow-tailed coat, white shirt, and tie, was anything but the nation's representative civilian magistrate. The crafty president, however, soon came to regard his plain attire as a potential advantage. "Black coats are at a discount in the presence of the blue," he admitted, "and I recognize the merit of the discount."

Attempts to crown Lincoln with allegorical glory seemed equally ill-advised. David Gilmour Blythe's painting, *Lincoln Crushing the Dragon of Rebellion*, for example, offered a president in homespun clothing suggestive of his prairie days. And Kimmel & Forster's print, *The Outbreak of the Rebellion*, confused the issue by suggesting that Lincoln's attempts to quash secession had been hampered by money-mad capitalists. Rather than attempt to live up to such grandiose interpretations, Lincoln confined himself to making every effort to show support for his soldiers. Accordingly, he doffed his hat to regiments as they marched past the

White House, and on several occasions traveled to the front to review troops in person.

Predictably, not everyone appreciated his appearances on the battlefield. One bold critic informed the president bluntly that "soldiers . . . write home to their friends . . . with reference to their disappointment in your bearing and manners when reviewing them." Lincoln should, the critic concluded, "consult somebody, some military man, as to what you ought to do on these occasions in military presence."

Fortunately for the president, however, such encounters between Lincoln and his troops were often sympathetically recorded for the illustrated weeklies by "special artists" assigned to cover the war. Alfred R. Waud sketched Lincoln, under the scrutiny of the 12th New York Volunteers, raising the American flag on the White House lawn; he also captured Lincoln's April 9, 1863, review of General Joseph Hooker's troops at Falmouth, Virginia. Photographer Alexander Gardner was present when Lincoln met with General George B. McClellan in October 1862 after the Battle of Antietam. In order to suggest the rough conditions of a military campaign, Gardner posed the two men meeting inside a tent. But these were exceptions. For the most part, Lincoln's wartime image remained almost wholly civilian and inexorably tied to the city of Washington.

This print, published during the 1864 presidential race, portrayed Lincoln soliciting votes among the dead and wounded on the Antietam battlefield.

In May 1862, Lincoln cruised to Hampton Roads, Virginia, and for a time actually assumed direct control of a Union action against the city of Norfolk. Secretary of the Treasury Salmon P. Chase, no great admirer of the president, was moved to admit: "I think it quite certain that if he had not come down, [Norfolk] would still have been in possession of the enemy."

In the months that followed, Lincoln seemed more impatient than ever with "procrastination on the part of commanders." Once, after learning that Confederate raiders had seized a Union general and twelve mules, he reacted sarcastically: "How unfortunate; I can fill his place with one of my generals in five minutes, but those mules cost us two hundred dollars apiece." And when the Army of the Potomac failed to follow its victory over Robert E. Lee at Gettysburg with the pursuit Lincoln believed could have ended the war, the president exploded: "If I had gone up there I could have whipped them myself."

But the commander in chief's only subsequent exposure to combat did not come until a year later, during the summer of 1864, when Jubal Early's troops threatened Washington. Climbing onto a parapet at Fort Stevens in nearby Maryland, his tall stovepipe hat an easy target for the enemy, Lincoln defiantly exposed himself to fire. To this display of raw courage, a horrified young officer named Oliver Wendell Holmes, Jr.—who would win fame years later as an associate justice of the U.S. Supreme Court—bellowed: "Get down you fool!"

Seeming to echo those sentiments, the image-makers refused to cloak Lincoln in soldierly glory. Equestrian portraits, which abounded in art of the period, routinely featured Jefferson Davis on horseback in classically heroic poses. Yet the closest that portraitists ever came to sitting Lincoln on a mount was during the 1860 presidential campaign, when Currier & Ives lampooned him as an organ grinder's monkey astride a hobbyhorse. In the more sophisticated view of Adalbert Volck, a pro-Confederate printmaker from Baltimore forced to publish his caricatures in secret, the best that could be said of Lincoln was that he was a modern version of the hapless Don Quixote, riding comically in search of his impossible dream. A Southern engraver presented Lincoln as a desperate puppet-master, forced to introduce his latest doll, "Fighting Joe" Hooker, after having shelved such previous failures as Ambrose Burnside and George B. McClellan.

Unfortunately for Lincoln, such criticism also came to him from Northern printmakers. Artist David H. Strother's series of drawings mocking McClellan's disastrous Peninsula campaign showed the president literally prodding the general into action at the sharp end of a bayonet. Although intended to criticize McClellan, the drawings also reminded viewers that Lincoln had fared no better in his role of commander in chief.

Printmakers did seem to sense that on January 1, 1863—the day that the Emancipation Proclamation took effect—Lincoln had unleashed the most powerful weapon of the entire war. The president gambled that the document would be more effective if crafted "as a war measure from the commander in chief of the army, but not on one issuing from the bosom of philanthropy." The response of printmakers showed that the strategy had worked to the president's advantage.

Dennis Malone Carter pictured Lincoln receiving a rousing welcome from the black and white residents of Richmond in the closing days of the war. In reality, only the newly freed Negroes turned out to greet the Great Emancipator.

Engravers and lithographers of the day sold their wares primarily to the same Americans to whom Lincoln had positioned the proclamation "as a war measure, and not a measure of morality." It was, therefore, in the printmakers' interest to avoid portraying the proclamation as an abolitionist decree, a tactic that might have made their pictures less appealing to buyers. Of the many images of Lincoln liberating grateful slaves that have become familiar to Americans, none was issued while the war still raged. Prints such as the one by Currier & Ives that portrayed the Emancipation Proclamation solely as a weapon designed for destroying the dragon of secession did provide Lincoln with some pictorial acclaim as the Union's commander in chief, but for his success with a pen, not a sword.

Vicious anti-Lincoln graphics abounded during the president's 1864 campaign for re-election. None hurt more than *The Commander in Chief Conciliating the Soldiers' Votes on the Battle Field*, a print that illustrated the libelous claim that a callous Lincoln had called for ribald songs as he walked among the dead and wounded following the Battle of Antietam.

Naturally, the presidential campaign of 1864 also featured positive images of the incumbent. Challenging Lincoln was George McClellan, a military man now incongruously running on a peace platform. Printmakers thus found it inviting to portray McClellan, not Lincoln, as a coward, lampooning him for allegedly observing battles from the safety of distant gunboats. It seemed just as natural for some image-makers to present Lincoln, armed with bayonet, personally repelling the threat to Union and liberty that McClellan now posed to America's future. Such prints did not fully recognize Lincoln as a military leader, but they moved his image closer in that direction than ever before.

Only after Lincoln fell victim to an assassin's bullet did a significant number of printmakers fully recognize his heretofore seldom-acknowledged role as commander in chief. Prints began showing him, together with General Ulysses S. Grant, as Columbia's Noblest Sons, or alongside the most famous of all general-presidents, George Washington, as "founder" and "preserver" of the Union. Currier & Ives issued its first council of war group, showing the president conferring, presumably on military strategy, with Generals Grant, William T. Sherman, and Philip H. Sheridan. Yet, even when the setting for such prints was moved outdoors, which a New York printmaker did for the 1865 lithograph, *Lincoln and His Generals*, the late president remained a symbol of civilian, not military, authority. Nonetheless, he was shown as the very center of attention, Admirals David D. Porter and David G. Farragut, together with Generals Sherman, Grant, Sheridan, and George H. Thomas, facing him in rapt attention. The scene was wholly imaginary, but seemed realistic enough to one photographer to inspire him to copy the print, re-title it *Lincoln and His Generals in Council Before Richmond* and issue the result as a *carte de visite*. The photographer's creation strongly suggested that Lincoln had personally devised the strategy that led to the capture of the Confederate capital.

Actually, Lincoln was indeed quite close to the scene of that surrender. On March 20, 1865, Grant had wired the president from his headquarters at City Point, Virginia: "Can you not visit . . . for a day or two?" On March 23, Lincoln journeyed south on the steamer *River Queen* and stayed for more than two weeks. It was his longest, and last, trip to the front.

A German lithographer may have come close to satisfying post-assassination public taste with a highly romanticized picture of Lincoln, now looking positively warlike on horseback as he rode triumphantly into City Point. The problem was that the print was misconceived. City Point was, by the time of Lincoln's arrival, a bustling Union supply center, not a bombed-out ruin, as this image suggested. No wounded soldiers filled its streets and no ex-slaves exulted at his arrival. Besides, Lincoln had come by ship, not on horseback. In all likelihood, the European printmaker had confused reports of Lincoln's final days in the field, mistaking City Point for the devastated Richmond. Ironically, the printmaker thus created, although for the wrong reasons, the kind of heroic equestrian picture with which Lincoln was never honored during his life.

The print certainly failed to suggest the eerily quiet entrance that

Lincoln ultimately made into the conquered capital city on April 4, 1865. There was no sign of military presence when Lincoln first stepped unannounced from a small boat onto Richmond's shores, accompanied only by a few soldiers and his son Tad, who clung tightly to his father's hand. For a time, Lincoln and his entourage walked in silence. Then, some black workmen suddenly recognized the president. With shouts of "Bless the Lord, there is the Great Messiah! . . . Glory, Hallelujah!" one of the newly liberated slaves boisterously heralded the arrival of the Great Emancipator. Minutes later, Lincoln was surrounded by a crush of well-wishers. "Such wild, indescribable joy I have never witnessed," wrote a newspaperman of the scene. Here was "the great deliverer, meeting the delivered."

Tears came to Lincoln's eyes as he made his way through the joyous crowd. One awed eyewitness quickly grasped the full meaning of what was the Union commander in chief's final military moment: "He came not as a conqueror, not with bitterness in his heart, but with kindness. He came as a friend, to alleviate sorrow and suffering—to rebuild what had been destroyed."

Harold Holzer is vice-president of communications at the Metropolitan Museum of Art. He is the author of many articles and books about Lincoln and the Civil War, including The Lincoln Image: Abraham Lincoln and the Popular Print.

John Wilkes Booth in his favorite role: the dashing actor. "My profession, my name, is my passport," he said.

2

Rebels with a Cause

JOHN WILKES BOOTH MIGHT HAVE GRUDGINGLY approved of Lincoln's regular invocations of Shakespeare, a genius both men revered, but certainly there was nothing else to recommend about the man he variously referred to as a tyrant, a Caesar, and "that big gorilla in the White House." As the war continued to go badly for the Confederacy in 1864, the actor's apprehension about the South's future became more acute and his schemes about personally doing something about it grew more grandiose. This was entirely in keeping with his personality, his older brother, Edwin, reflected years later. "He was a rattle-pated fellow," he said, "filled with Quixotic notions."

As a boy, John Wilkes had charged on horseback through the woods on the family farm in Maryland, spouting heroic speeches with an old lance, a relic of the Mexican War, in his hand. "We regarded him as a good-hearted, harmless, though wild-brained boy, and used to laugh at his patriotic froth whenever secession was discussed," said Edwin. "That he was insane on that one point, no one who knew him well can doubt."

The loyalty of family members to the Union riled John Wilkes, to the point that the Booths tried not to discuss politics when together. When Edwin admitted in the fall of 1864 that he had voted for Lincoln—*again*—John Wilkes "expressed deep regret, and declared his belief that Lincoln would be made king of America." This, Edwin believed, drove his brother "beyond the limits of reason."

★

Questionable sanity, political activism, and a love of drama—both real and staged—were the threads that connected the Booths of the Old World to those of the New. In the early 1700s, John Wilkes Booth's ancestors had been thrown out of Portugal for their radical views. Landing in London, the Booths became admirers of John Wilkes, the liberty-loving Lord Mayor of London. Wilkes was outspoken in his opposition to the power of King George III and unceasing in his championing of civil rights.

One of Wilkes' relatives was Richard Booth. During the American Revolution, he wanted to sail to America and join the colonists in their struggle for independence. Stopped in mid-ocean and returned to England, he had to settle for hanging a portrait of George Washington in the parlor of his London home and demanding that visitors bow to it before entering.

From the beginning, all Booths displayed an almost frightening admiration of "those illustrious worthys, Brutus and Cassius," as Richard Booth once described the toga-clad heroes of republicanism. His son, the brilliant and eccentric Shakesperean actor Junius Brutus Booth, made his reputation playing them in such classics as *Julius Caesar* and *Brutus*.

Junius Brutus Booth, Sr. The father of John Wilkes Booth was a leading actor in his day and known as an eccentric genius of the stage. John Wilkes was fourteen when he died.

By his early twenties Junius was being favorably compared to Edmund Kean, England's leading tragedian. Arguments by their respective supporters often led to fist fights in the audience during performances. In 1821, twenty-five-year-old Junius settled the debate over who was the finest actor in England by sailing to the United States and quickly becoming the finest actor in America. He took along a pretty flower girl named Mary Ann Holmes, who happened to be at least the third woman he had impregnated. That he left behind a wife and son in England concerned Junius not a whit.

Junius and his mistress settled in the woods near Bel Air, Maryland. Together they had ten children, four of whom died in infancy. Of those that survived, three brothers—Edwin, Junius, Jr., and John Wilkes—ignored their father's wishes and followed him onto the stage. Their collective contribution as actors and managers made the Booths the first family of the American theater.

The talent and eccentricities of "Booth the Elder" made him the most colorful actor of his time, a must-see in New York, Baltimore, Savannah, Charleston, Petersburg, New Orleans, and other major venues. Once, during a tour of coastal cities, he impulsively jumped off a steamer into the ocean, later claiming to his rescuers that he'd been carrying a message for a drowned actor named Conway. As that incident demonstrated, whiskey was a problem. It was anybody's call whether Junius would show up for a show drunk or sober; in either state, he could be counted on to give a vigorous, passionate performance. His sword duels regularly drew blood and often carried over from the stage into the audience and, on more than once occasion, out the door and up the street. Short, stocky, and unapologetically bellicose, he thought nothing of stopping a play in mid-sentence, stomping to the footlights, and cussing out an inattentive or gossipy member of the audience. His belligerence could be costly; he once caught a poker in the face, which permanently flattened his nose.

Because of the public nature of their profession, it behooved actors to keep their political opinions to themselves. Nonetheless, Junius's radicalism sometimes burst into the open. Indignant over the impending execution of a notorious horse thief whose cause he had taken up, he sent several inflammatory letters to President Andrew Jackson. One read:

Through the centuries, stage plays often vilified tyrants and glorified political assassination. This playbill advertises a performance of Junius Booth, Sr., in two examples: Richard III *and* Killing No Murder.

You damn'd old Scoundrel if you don't sign the pardon of your fellow men now under sentence of Death . . . I will cut your throat whilst you are sleeping. I wrote you repeated Cautions, so look out or damn you I'll have you burnt at the Stake in the City of Washington.

Your Master
Junius Brutus Booth

You know me! Look out!

The execution took place anyway. In appreciation of Junius's efforts, the doomed man arranged to have his skull mailed to him for use in performances of *Hamlet*.

MR. BOOTH,

AS BRUTUS.

Engraved by G.B.Ellis from a Painting by J.Neagle.
Lopez and Wemyss Edition

Junius Brutus Booth, Jr., was John Wilkes' oldest brother and the eldest of ten children. He was a prominent actor and theater manager. Like most actors of his time, Junius played Brutus on occasion. The assassin of Julius Caesar was a great hero to the Booths, as Junius's middle name attests.

The "Mad Booths of Maryland" grew by one when John Wilkes Booth was born on May 10, 1838. He was named after his ancestor, the famous English radical reformer. Technically, he was a bastard, a fact that shamed him tremendously when the existence of his father's other family became a public scandal. Junius Booth waited until John Wilkes' thirteenth birthday in 1851 before divorcing his English wife and then legally marrying Mary Ann.

While Junius was alive, the Booth children enjoyed a freewheeling, if somewhat unconventional, lifestyle. Summers

Tudor Hall, the home of the Maryland Booths, is now a bed and breakfast. It stands three miles east of Bel Air, Maryland.

were spent on the Maryland farm, which eventually was supplanted by an English-style country home, Tudor Hall. (Ironically, the man who built Tudor Hall, James Johnson Gifford, later built Ford's Theater.) The rest of the year the family stayed at a house in Baltimore, about twenty-fives miles away.

When he wasn't into the whiskey, Junius could be a gentle and indulgent soul. Not only did he forbid his children from hunting or chopping down trees, he was known to hold Christian burials for dead birds and animals. It was true that he occasionally used Negroes for work around the farm, but he always borrowed them from neighbors. He was never a slave-owner, and in fact assisted some in buying their freedom. These kinds of attitudes marked him as unusual in the eyes of his possum-hunting, slaveowning neighbors.

John Wilkes (who often was called Johnny or Wilkes by family members and friends) was schooled in the finest private academies, where he studied the works of Shakespeare, Milton, and Plutarch. However, in November 1852, Junius Booth died aboard a Mississippi steamboat while returning from a western tour with Junius, Jr., and Edwin. This forced John Wilkes to end his classical education at fourteen and become the man of the house while his older brothers were away.

Strapped for cash, the family soon sold the Baltimore house and moved permanently to Tudor Hall. There John Wilkes became soulmates with his older sister, Asia, a smart, pretty, and passionate girl who wound up writing several books about her famous family. Close in age and sharing similar interests in poetry, nature, and music, the two siblings were "lonely together," as Asia put it. They fished, dug for Indian relics, explored the countryside on foot and by horse, and whiled away time just talking. "We spent many hours of the long summer afternoons under the widest-spreading trees," she recalled, "reading aloud from Byron's poems; or seated together in the broad swing under the gum trees and hickories, we would build fantastic temples of fame that were to resound with his name in the days that were coming."

A family friend once observed that "patriotic fervor was the ruling passion" of the Booths. From Portugal to England to America, the Booths had always demonstrated an intense dislike for authoritarian rule and a love of equality. On this last point John Wilkes strayed from his ancestral roots. His view was that blacks and foreign-born whites were inferiors. It was the conventional belief held by Marylanders in the tumultuous 1850s, as the Know-Nothing Party attempted to stem the tide of immigrants then flooding America's shores. The issue of "nativism," then, became John Wilkes' first political cause, even though he was too young to vote.

"The first evidence of an undemocratic feeling in Wilkes was shown when we were expected to sit down with our hired workmen," Asia wrote of her brother's early experiences supervising the harvest at Tudor Hall:

> It was the custom for members of the family to dine and sup with the white men who did the harvesting. Wilkes had a struggle with his pride and knew not which to abide by, his love

Edwin Booth, today considered one of the finest actors America ever produced, is shown here in his most notable role, Hamlet.

of equality and brotherhood, or that southern reservation which jealously kept the white laborer from free association with his employer or his superior. His father would not have hesitated a instant, nor would Richard Booth, the rebel-patriot grandfather, have considered the matter twice. The difference between the impassioned self-made Republican and the native-born southern American is wide. One overlaps restraint by his enthusiasm, desiring to cast off at a swoop the trammels of a former allegiance, and is over eager to fraternize with all men; but the other cautiously creates for himself a barrier called respect, with which he fences off familiarity and its concomitant evils. This made the master a god in the South, to be either loved or feared. There were no "Masters" and "Mistresses" in the North.

John Wilkes' compromise was to sit down and eat with the soiled and sunburned workers, but without the women of the household present. His distaste for existing alongside "darkies" and commoners grew over the next couple of years and undoubtedly made his decision to attempt a career in the theater an easier one. He was barely seventeen when, in August of 1855, he made his acting debut at Baltimore's Charles Street Theater playing the Earl of Richmond in *Richard III*. The role was made to order for a Booth; in the play, Richmond overthrows the detestable despot. The youngster was a last-minute substitute for an actor who had fallen ill; afterward it was back to Tudor Hall, where his mother tried to convince him to consider a different line of work.

The three Booth brothers of the stage as they appeared in Julius Caesar *on November 25, 1864. From left: John Wilkes as Mark Antony, Edwin as Brutus, and Junius, Jr., as Cassius.*

Asia's marriage to the comedic actor John Sleeper Clarke, followed by their move into an old mansion in Philadelphia, provided the break John Wilkes needed. In 1857, his brother-in-law got him into the stock company of the Arch Street Theater, where for eight dollars a week "Mr. Wilks" performed a variety of roles. The following theatrical season found him in

Richmond, performing as "J.B. Wilkes." By 1860, he was chewing the scenery in places like Montgomery, Alabama and Columbus, Georgia.

The boy hungered to make a name for himself, like his father had, but he lacked Junius Booth's natural talent. He was raw and untrained, but he possessed certain qualities that compensated. He was handsome, boasting thick dark hair and the large and expressive hazel eyes of his mother. He stood about five feet, seven inches tall, albeit on a pair of extremely bowed legs. He had a compact, athletic build—perfect for swashbuckling swordplay and acrobatic leaps about the stage—and could be devastatingly charming, particularly around women.

Booth was a sexual scamp, sleeping with a variety of actresses, prostitutes, and theater groupies. One scorned lover stabbed herself in a fit after a show in Albany in 1861. Before too long he was exchanging valentines with Lucy Hale, the dark, plump daughter of New Hampshire Senator John Hale. But that didn't stop his relationship with countless others, including his favorite: a diminutive redhead named Ella Turner, who stayed at her sister's brothel when the dashing actor was unable to entertain her inside his Washington hotel room.

Although he would always have trouble remembering his lines and would never match his brother Edwin's flair for conveying pathos and suspense, by the beginning of the war John Wilkes Booth was proven "box office." His performances tended to be better received by critics and playgoers in what were known as "the provinces"—Albany, Louisville, Cincinnati—than in the big Eastern cities of New York, Boston, and Philadelphia, where reputations were made. He was a popular, if not always a critical, success. While a writer for the populist *Spirit of the Times* described him as "an actor of genius and talent, with the capacity of becoming very great in the more tempestuous sort of tragedy and melodrama," the influential New York critic William Winter sniffed that Booth was "raw, crude, and much given to boisterous declamation."

The criticism stung Booth, who the press often found wanting when compared to his famous father and more accomplished brother. Craving fame, he was instead becoming notorious for his drinking, womanizing, and uneven performances. One of Booth's childhood friends later said that it was a "name in history" that the actor most desperately desired. "A glorious career he thought of by day and dreamed of by night. He always said he would 'make his name remembered by succeeding generations.' "

★

Because of the lofty position Lincoln holds in American history and folklore, it has been generally forgotten how hated he was as president; in fact, he was easily the most reviled of all chief executives. He was considered an ogre by Southerners, but his exercising of emergency powers during the war also had many in the North denouncing him as well. The draft, arbitrary arrests, the confiscation of slaves from suspected Rebels—all were measures that, though ultimately approved by Congress, raised the hackles of lovers of personal liberty. Editorials in Southern papers regularly referred to Lincoln as a Caesar and drew parallels between modern and ancient times. Some called for the president's abduction—or worse. "Assassination in the abstract is a horrid crime," reasoned one Richmond newspaper, "and so is every kind of killing; but to slay a tyrant is no more assassination than war is murder. Who speaks of Brutus as an assassin?" A businessman in Alabama ran an advertisement offering $1 million to whoever killed the president.

Lincoln, characteristically fatalistic, shrugged off the many threats that passed through the War Department. If nothing else, he reckoned that he had history on his side. Political assassination was practically unheard of in the young republic, although there had been at least one attempt on a president's life. In 1835, the same year Booth's father had threatened to kill Andrew Jackson in Washington, a deranged English house painter named Samuel Lawrence tried to do just that. As Jackson stepped out onto the portico of the Hall of Representatives after a state funeral, Lawrence rushed at him with two pistols. Beating what one firearms expert later determined were 1-in-125,000 odds, both pistols misfired. "Ol' Hickory," still feisty at sixty-eight, started whacking Lawrence with his cane before the unlucky assailant was handcuffed and led off. Lawrence eventually was judged criminally insane for claiming that Jackson had deprived him from becoming the king of England.

Booth's regularly voiced concern was that Lincoln—a man whose appearance, upbringing, and policies utterly disgusted him—would ultimately overthrow the Constitution and become "king of America." He had seen firsthand the power of the government in crushing dissent. In 1859, he was appearing in Richmond when word came of John Brown's raid on the federal arsenal at Harper's Ferry, Virginia (now West Virginia). Brown and his supporters had hoped to instigate and arm a slave revolt, but U.S. Marines under the command of Colonel Robert E. Lee captured the abolitionist and several followers after a bloody shootout. When Brown was hanged on December 2, 1859, Booth was there at the foot of the scaffold, outfitted in a uniform hastily borrowed from members of the Richmond Grays, the militia group assigned to keep order.

Although Booth was impressed by Brown's courage, on that occasion he had sided with the government. Not so in April 1861, when federal troops marching through Baltimore on their way to Washington were attacked by a mob of Southern sympathizers. The ensuing riot, in which twelve civilians were killed, prompted Lincoln to suspend the writ of habeas corpus and place the city under martial law. Lincoln realized that it was strategically critical that Maryland, a largely pro-Southern state that practically surrounded Washington, be kept in the Union. Maryland remained a star on the flag, though it came at the expense of due process. For the duration of the war Marylanders suspected of being "secesh" were routinely seized and tossed in jail. Court orders were ignored and judges intimidated. With just weeks on the job, the man accustomed to tugging snug boots over his size-fifteen feet was similarly stretching the traditionally narrow limits of his office.

Booth, a crack pistol shot, also was known for his leaps and acrobatics on stage, but upon the outbreak of war the physically fit twenty-two-year-old refrained from enlisting in the Rebel ranks or making good on his boast to raise a militia unit. At one point Edwin asked his brother why he didn't join the Confederate army, to which he replied: "I promised mother I would keep out of the quarrel, if possible, and I am sorry that I said so." Some whispered that he had an inordinate fear of having his face scarred in battle.

Throughout the war that face allowed him to move freely, though the fighting forced him to confine his performances to Northern cities. "My face is my passport," he boasted, but he was feeling increasingly guilty about his contribution to the cause, particularly as conditions worsened in 1864. While starving, underequipped soldiers were dying in such godforsaken places as the Wilderness, he was still enjoying the high life. At a time when thousands of men his age were fighting as virgins, he had access to sweethearts and soft featherbeds in hotels all over the map. That year he again made $20,000, more than double what the revered Robert E. Lee was receiving for battling the Union war machine to a standstill. Privates got a pay raise to $18 a month; the nearly worthless Confederate currency made it equal to about a dollar in gold.

Booth's angst is apparent in a letter he wrote his mother shortly after Lincoln's re-election: "For four years I have lived (I may say) a *slave* in the North (a favored slave it's true, but no less hateful to me on that account), not daring to express my thoughts or sentiments, even in my home, constantly hearing every principle dear to my heart denounced as treasonable, and knowing the vile and savage acts committed on my countrymen, their wives, and helpless children, that I have cursed my wilful idleness, and begun to deem myself a coward and to despise my own existence."

The letter, discovered a couple of days after the assassination, asked for his mother's understanding and forgiveness for releasing himself from his pledge. He had placed it, along with several other documents, inside the safe at his sister's Philadelphia mansion either in late 1864 or early 1865.

A longer and far more revealing letter was found with it. For lack of a better description, it can be called Booth's "manifesto," a rambling note to the world that he hoped would, in the event of his death, explain his rationale behind the great deed that he had decided to devote the next few months of his life to: *capturing*—not killing—President Lincoln.

> MY DEAR SIR: You may use this as you think best. But as *some* may wish to know *when, who,* and *why,* and as I know not *how* to direct, I give it (in the words of your master)

Inauguration day, March 4, 1865.

"To whom it may concern:"

Right or wrong, God judge me, not man. For be my motive good or bad, of one thing I am sure, the lasting condemnation of the North.

I love peace more than life. Have loved the Union beyond expression. For four years have I waited, hoped, and prayed for the dark clouds to break, and for a restoration of our former sunshine. To wait longer would be a crime. All hope for peace is dead. My prayers have proved as idle as my hopes. God's will be done. I go to see and share the bitter end.

I have ever held the South were right. The very nomination

Scenes from a devastated South in the closing months of the war: A pockmarked mansion in Atlanta and a ruined locomotive depot in Richmond.

of Abraham Lincoln, four years ago, spoke plainly war—war upon Southern rights and institutions. His election proved it. "Await an overt act." Yes, till you are bound and plundered. What folly! The South were wise. Who thinks of arguments or patience when the finger of his enemy presses on the trigger? In a *foreign* war, I, too, could say, "Country, right or wrong." But in a struggle *such as ours* (where the brother tries to pierce the brother's heart), for God's sake choose the right. When a country like this spurns *justice* from her side she forfeits the allegiance of every honest freeman and should leave him, untrammelled by any fealty soever, to act as his conscience may approve. People of the North, to hate tyranny, to love liberty and justice, to strike at wrong and oppression, was the teaching of our fathers. The study of our early history will not let me forget it, and may it never.

This country was formed for the *white*, not for the black man. And, looking upon *African slavery* from the same standpoint held by the noble framers of our Constitution, I, for one, have ever considered it one of the greatest blessings (both for themselves and us) that God ever bestowed upon a favored nation. Witness heretofore our wealth and power; witness their elevation and enlightenment above their race elsewhere. I have lived among it most of my life, and have seen *less* harsh treatment from master to man than I have beheld in the North from father to son. Yet, Heaven knows, *no one* would be willing to do more for the negro race than I, could I but see a way to *still better their condition*. But Lincoln's policy is only preparing a way for their total annihilation. The South *are not, nor have they been, fighting* for the continuation of slavery. The first battle of Bull Run did away with that idea. Their causes *since* for *war* have been as *noble* and *greater far than those that urged our fathers on*. Even should we allow they were wrong at the beginning of this contest, *cruelty and injustice* have made the wrong become *the right*, and they stand now (before the wonder and admiration of the world) as a noble band of patriotic heroes. Hereafter, reading of *their deeds*, Thermopylae will be forgotten.

When I aided in the capture and execution of John Brown (who was a murderer on our western border and who was fairly *tried* and *convicted* before an impartial judge and jury, of treason, and who, by the way, has since been made a god) I was proud of my little share in the transaction, for I deemed it my duty, and that I was helping our common country to perform an act of justice. But what was a crime in poor John Brown is now considered (by themselves) as the greatest and only virtue of the whole Republican party. Strange transmigration! *Vice* to become a *virtue*, simply because *more* indulge in it!

I thought then, *as now*, that the Abolitionists were *the only traitors* in the land and that the entire party deserved the same fate as poor old Brown, not because they wished to abolish slavery, but on account of the means they have ever endeavored to use to effect that abolition. If Brown were living I doubt whether he *himself* would set slavery against the Union. Most, or many in the North do, and openly curse the Union, if the

Several members of the 107th U.S. Colored Infantry, which saw action late in the war. To John Wilkes Booth and many other Southerners, perhaps the most galling aspect of the Confederacy's impending defeat was the presence of tens of thousands of black soldiers in the Union ranks. "This country was formed for the white man," Booth fumed, "not for the black."

South are to return and retain a *single right* guaranteed to them by every tie which we once revered as *sacred*. The South can make no choice. It is either extermination or slavery for *themselves* (worse than death) to draw from. I know *my* choice. I have also studied hard to know upon what grounds the right of a State to secede has been denied, when our very name, United States, and the Declaration of Independence, *both* provide for secession.

But there is no time for words. I write in haste. I know how foolish I shall be deemed for taking such a step as this, where, on the one side, I have many friends and everything to make me happy, where my profession *alone* has gained me an income of *more than* twenty thousand dollars a year, and where my great personal ambition in my profession has such a great field

A detail from one of the photographs taken at Lincoln's second inauguration reveals how close his future assassin (identified by arrow) was able to get. Just below Booth is his good friend, theater owner John Ford.

for labor. On the other hand, the South have never bestowed upon me one kind word: a place now where I have no friends, except beneath the sod; where I must either become a private soldier or a beggar. To give up all of the *former* for the *latter*, besides my mother and my sisters whom I love so dearly (although they so widely differ from me in opinion) seems insane; but God is my judge. I love *justice* more than I do a country that disowns it; more than fame and wealth; more (Heaven pardon me if wrong), more than a happy home.

I have never been upon a battlefield; but oh! my country-men, could you all but see the *reality* or effects of this horrid war, as I have seen them (in *every State*, save Virginia,) I know you would think like me, and would pray the Almighty to cre-ate in the Northern mind a sense of *right and justice* (even should it possess no seasoning of mercy) and that He would dry up the sea of blood between us, which is daily growing wider. Alas! poor country, is she to meet her threatened doom?

Four years ago I would have given a thousand lives to see her remain (as I had always known her) powerful and unbro-ken. And even now I would hold my life as naught to see her what she was. Oh! my friends, if the fearful scenes of the past four years had never been enacted, or if what has been had been but a frightful dream from which we could now awake, with what overflowing hearts could we bless our God and pray for His continued favor! How I have loved the *old flag* can never now be known. A few years since and the entire world could boast of none so pure and spotless. But I have of late been see-ing and hearing of the *bloody deeds* of which she has *been made the emblem*, and would shudder to think how changed she had grown. Oh! how I have longed to see her break from the mist of blood that circles round her folds, spoiling her beauty, and tarnishing her honor. But no, day by day has she been dragged deeper and deeper into cruelty and oppression, till now (in my eyes) her once bright red stripes look like *bloody gashes* on the face of Heaven. I look now upon my early admiration of her glories as a dream. My love (as things stand today) is for the South alone. Nor do I deem it a dishonor in attempting to make for her a prisoner of this man, to whom she owes so much of misery.

If success attends me, I go penniless to her side. They say

she has found that "last ditch" which the North has so long derided, and been endeavoring to force her in, forgetting they are our brothers, and that it is impolitic to goad an enemy to madness. Should I reach her in safety and find it true, I will proudly beg permission to triumph or die in that same "ditch" by her side.

A Confederate doing duty upon his own responsibility.

J. WILKES BOOTH

"To whom it may concern" was an obvious dig at Lincoln's recent executive order (which began with that rude salutation) regarding *New York Tribune* publisher Horace Greeley's failed peace negotiations with Confederate representatives in Canada.

Booth's penchant for exaggeration and self-aggrandizement is evident throughout. He had not taken part in the capture of John Brown, and his claim that the South had never bestowed "one kind word" upon him also was untrue. The final sentence indicates that he was not acting as the agent of the Confederate government. Whether this was the truth, deliberate disinformation, or simply an attempt to grab sole credit for what he proposed to do remains an open question. In any event, as fellow actor William Seymour later observed, "The signs of insanity are in this letter."

Lucy Lambert Hale, born in 1842, was the daughter of former New Hampshire senator John P. Hale, who in 1865 was appointed minister to Spain by Lincoln. Lucy Hale was the love of John Wilkes Booth's life—or so he professed. When Booth was killed, the photographs of four other women were found on his person.

★

The notion that the president could be captured was not a hare-brained one. In fact, in 1864 the Confederate high command launched at least two secret-service operations designed to nab Lincoln, but both fizzled. The idea was always alive, however, and it was especially appealing to Booth, who in the summer of 1864 had suffered a personal loss. His best friend, a childhood chum named Jesse Wharton, died inside a Union jail. Wharton represented just one of thousands of soldiers on both sides who died in captivity of starvation, disease, and abuse. The issue of captives was especially sensitive to both governments, now that papers were printing the details of hellholes like Andersonville and Libby Prison and the North had ended its policy of prisoner exchanges. Booth's plan was to snatch Lincoln and hold him hostage until the North agreed to resume swapping prisoners, thus freeing badly needed manpower to the thinning ranks of the Confederacy.

What was behind Booth's call to action? Guilt over not having contributed more to the cause? His genuine hatred of Lincoln? His ancestral love of liberty and drama? A desire to avenge the death of his friend? His sincere belief that he could alter the course of the war? Any or all of these may have entered into it. It's also hard to resist the feeling that overriding all of these noble considerations was the urge, prevalent since childhood, to be famous in his own lifetime—or, should he die in the attempt, to be hailed throughout his beloved South as a martyr.

There is no doubt that the kidnaping-turned-assassination of Lincoln was the product of a conspiracy. The mystery concerns its complexity. Was Booth operating on his own initiative? Or were he and his accomplices part of a grander scheme hatched in the upper levels of the Confederate government?

Booth, whose vocation allowed him to travel throughout the North and occupied cities of the South, had probably been doing favors for the Confederate "underground" since the spring of 1863, when he made the acquaintance of an immature, star-struck drugstore clerk in Washington named David Herold. Booth confided in his sister, Asia, how he smuggled quinine, an antimalarial medicine desperately needed by the Confederacy, inside the wide sleeves and deep pockets of his fashionably oversized coats. His custom-made riding boots also had pockets sewn into them—perfect for delivering mail. He told stories about nights spent in rowboats and laughed about the traveling pass, signed by General Grant; the commander had unwittingly provided him with "freedom of range without knowing what a good turn he has done the South." Despite these occasional displays of dash and derring-do, that Booth was an operative working for the Confederate secret service has never been conclusively proven.

Booth had already interested Herold and two longtime friends, both former Confederate soldiers, in his plot. Samuel Arnold had been friends with Jesse Wharton, while Michael

O'Laughlen, who had grown up across the street from Booth in Baltimore, had spent time as a prisoner of war.

It's not clear whether Booth knew of the two previous attempts to capture Lincoln, but his own plan was similar. He would grab the president while he was on his way to his summer retreat near the Soldiers' Home, a couple of miles from

the White House, then spirit him across the Anacostia River into southern Maryland, an area filled with Confederate sympathizers eager to help. Then it would be across the lower Potomac into Virginia for the final delivery to authorities in Richmond, at which point Jefferson Davis himself was sure to shake Booth's hand.

However, the high command had to be aware of what was going on. In October 1864, Booth met in Montreal with the "Canadian Cabinet," a group of Rebels whose mission was launching covert actions from across the border. Booth returned to southern Maryland with a letter of introduction that led to his meeting a local physician, Dr. Samuel A. Mudd. Booth, scouting escape routes under the guise of looking for

Two members of Booth's action team were George Atzerodt (left), a wagon painter who in his spare time ferried Confederate spies across the Potomac, and David Herold, an immature pharmacist's clerk. Their involvement with Booth would cause both men to be hanged.

some land to buy, wound up spending the night at Mudd's farm. By the time he joined his family in Philadelphia in mid-November, Booth had accumulated contacts—including a tough, clever agent named Thomas Harbin—and a rough idea of his avenue of escape.

Then it was on to New York, where on November 25, 1864, he joined brothers Edwin and Junius, Jr., for the first and only time together on stage at the Winter Garden for a benefit performance of *Julius Caesar*. Coincidentally or not, that evening Confederate agents set fire to thirteen hotels, including the one adjoining the theater. It was an attempt, admitted an arsonist hanged for his participation, to bring the war home to the fat and comfortable North. While in New York, Booth bought some knives and Spencer carbines and had them shipped to Sam Arnold in Baltimore, who was to then get them to Washington.

By the end of 1864 Booth had quit the stage and began to put his personal affairs into order. He continued cobbling together his action team and making preparations for the day they could get at Lincoln. He booked a room at Washington's National Hotel, close by Ford's Theater. Booth was good friends with the owner, John T. Ford, and knew nearly everybody connected with the theater. He had Edman "Ned" Spangler, a stage carpenter, convert a rented shack in the alley behind the theater into a stable for his three horses and a wagon. Over the winter and into spring, Spangler and errand boy John "Peanuts" Burroughs looked after them for Booth.

At some point it was suggested that Booth add John Surratt, a former divinity student turned Confederate courier, to the team. Dr. Mudd, in Washington doing some holiday shopping, introduced the men to each other a couple of days before Christmas. Soon Booth became a familiar face at the Washington boarding house operated by Surratt's middle-aged mother, which stood at 541 H Street, just a few blocks from Booth's hotel.

Mary Surratt also owned a tavern at Surrattsville, a crossroads about thirteen miles from Washington and named after her recently deceased husband, the local postmaster. Mrs. Surratt, in financial straits upon becoming a widow, had rented the tavern to a chronic alcoholic named John Lloyd and moved into the city. Her Confederate sympathies were no secret; she regularly harbored agents making their way through the area. Booth and his growing band of conspirators felt comfortable gathering under her roof and discussing abduction plans.

In January 1865, two new members were recruited. George Atzerodt, a German immigrant with a thick accent, was a carriage painter by day and blockade runner by night. He lived near Port Tobacco, Maryland, widely known as a smuggling haven. Atzerodt's job description was caretaker and navigator of the boat that would be pulled out of hiding at the proper moment and then used to transport the men and their prize across the river into Virginia. The job description for the other newcomer could be simply summed up as "muscle." Lewis Powell, a twenty-year-old veteran of several campaigns, was a big, bull-necked native of Alabama who had been wounded at Gettysburg and fought with the legendary Mosby's Rangers before being paroled as "Lewis Paine," just one of his many aliases. He boarded briefly at Mary Surratt's boardinghouse, where he posed as "Reverend Wood."

Putting the pieces together was costing Booth almost every dollar he had. Over the winter of 1864–65 he spent more than $10,000 on supplies, weapons, horses, a boat, and a wagon, not to mention his biggest expense: providing meals, drinks, lodging, and entertainment for the plotters while they loafed around Washington, waiting for the main chance.

Samuel Arnold, an ex-Confederate soldier and former schoolmate of Booth's, bought into his old friend's plan to abduct the president.

Idleness was becoming expensive and every day brought the Confederacy that much closer to final defeat. On March 4, 1865, Booth and Lucy Hale attended Lincoln's inauguration ceremony, thanks to tickets provided by Senator Hale. Kidnaping was still the plan at this stage, but Booth admitted later to how easy it would have been to kill the king of America, if he had wanted.

What Booth desired was, naturally, more dramatic. Pointing out that Lincoln rarely traveled to the Soldiers' Home anymore, he formulated an alternate plan whereby the president would be taken prisoner inside his box at Ford's Theater. At a signal, the gas lights would be extinguished and the president chloroformed, tied up, and lowered by rope to the stage, from where he would be rushed through the darkness into a waiting carriage. He went so far as to obtain tickets for Powell and

Surratt one evening so they could join him in casing the presidential box and figuring out the logistics involved. When this scheme was laid out in an oysters-and-champagne dinner for the action team on the evening of March 16, Samuel Arnold drunkenly called the idea suicide.

"You can be the leader of the party," he exclaimed, "but not my executioner!"

After more heated words, Booth agreed to return to the original plan.

The following day Booth learned from theatrical friends that Lincoln was scheduled to attend a play early that afternoon at Campbell Hospital, just north of Washington. After months of talking and plotting, now was the time for the action team to act! They would take the president as he rode back to the White House.

While John Surratt rented a large buggy, David Herold rushed to Surratt's Tavern with several weapons, and George Atzerodt readied the boat in the marshes, the others waited, their adrenaline pumping, in a tavern near the hospital. Finally, Booth rode out to see what was delaying the arrival of the president. Lincoln wasn't in attendance, he was told. As a matter of fact, at that very moment he was at Booth's hotel, the National, accepting a captured Confederate flag.

It was a humiliating fiasco. The next evening, March 18, as some of the conspirators were making up their minds to leave Washington and others wondered if their benefactor would continue to subsidize their stay, their ringleader played Pescara in *The Apostate* at Ford's Theater. It was Booth's last performance on stage, at least in costume. Time, like his temper, was growing short.

Was Booth Part of a Confederate Conspiracy?

⊰ BY WILLIAM A. TIDWELL ⊱

CONTRARY TO POPULAR BELIEF, the Lincoln assassination was *not* the act of a simple conspiracy; it was the result of a legitimate Confederate clandestine operation that went awry. In my opinion, conventional explanations of the president's murder are based largely on myth and were influenced by the need to smooth over bitter feelings generated by the Civil War. By blaming the assassination on John Wilkes Booth, acting alone, people on both sides of the conflict could agree that Lincoln's death was a tragedy for all and get on with the business of restoring a splintered, war-weary nation. This approach proved good for the country's healing but bad for historical scholarship. It has meant that, until recently, there has been no attempt by trained scholars to investigate what actually happened.

Over the last decade a large amount of documented evidence has been published that presents a radically different picture of the assassination. This evidence has not yet been assimilated by many in the academic community, but a brief review of it here will help the reader understand its significance in deflating century-old myths.

The first point to consider is the existence and organization of Confederate secret service activity. In the past many Confederate partisans denied any such activity, or at best allowed that any reference to the Confederate secret service concerned only the procurement of ships and weapons abroad. If the Confederacy had no secret service, the argument went, how could it have been involved in something as complicated as political assassination?

The answer can be found in the Library of Congress, where the papers of the Confederate States of America are housed. Among the documents are sixty-three vouchers, signed by Confederate President Jefferson Davis, calling for the allocation of gold to various secret service projects. They cover the period from August 1862 to March 1865 and involve the allocation of more than $1.5 million in gold, an immense sum for that period. Included in that amount was $1 million given to Jacob Thompson, the Confederate commissioner in Canada, to be used to stimulate support for the Copperhead peace movement in the North.

From these records and the remnants of a secret service record book now owned by the Chicago Historical Society, one learns that the Confederate Congress appropriated $840,000 for a secret service account known as "necessities and exigencies" and $5 million for an account known simply as "secret service." This latter account was established in early 1864 to support a program of active sabotage and other clandestine operations against the Union. The money was drawn by writing a request to Jefferson Davis outlining the purposes for which it was needed. If Davis approved of the project he signed a request to the Treasury, asking them to issue a warrant for the funds and specifying the secret service account that was to be used. These requests are the sixty-three vouchers found in the Library of Congress. The paperwork involved in the process was handled by Judah Benjamin, the Confederacy's secretary of state; the money was actually disbursed by Benjamin or a State Department clerk.

From these records, then, it is clear that Jefferson Davis kept personal control of the gold used for secret service purposes and that Judah Benjamin was familiar with the Confederacy's program of clandestine operations.

After Lincoln's assassination, the U.S. government set out to prove that the murder was the work of the Confederacy and used the trial of Booth's associates to try to make its case. However, during the conspiracy trial of 1865 the government had at their disposal nowhere near the amount of material that is available today. Since then the National Archives and other repositories have collected and organized a great quantity of information bearing on the Civil War, and that includes material that pertains to the assassination.

In addition to being hampered by a lack of evidence, the Union prosecutors made a mistake in tactics. In 1864 the Confederacy initiated a clandestine operation to capture Lincoln and hold him as a hostage. John Wilkes Booth appears to have been recruited as the man to carry out the plan. There is ample evidence of Booth's role as the leader of the action team. However, prosecutors tried to present evidence of this hostage effort as a cover for a long-existing Confederate plan to assassinate the president.

To thwart this, the Confederates who had been managing clandestine operations from Canada managed to insert witnesses into the trial who swore to the guilt of the South, but who were easily exposed as perjurers. The case against the Confederacy collapsed and its operation to capture Lincoln was never again publicly scrutinized. As a result, the American public was left believing that the Confederacy had never taken any action against Lincoln.

In actuality, Booth and his associates had tried to capture Lincoln

Actor . . . smuggler . . . Confederate operative?

on March 17, 1865, but a change in the president's plans frustrated their effort. After that, there was never another chance to capture him. A series of later actions, all well documented, support the conclusion that the Confederacy then adopted a radically different course of action.

On April 10, 1865, near Burke Station, Virginia, just fifteen miles from Washington, Union cavalry skirmished with a detachment of Colonel John S. Mosby's 43rd Regiment of Virginia Cavalry. A Confederate sergeant named Thomas F. Harney was captured. Upon interrogation, Harney claimed to be from the Engineer Bureau of the Confederate War Department and had recently delivered "ordnance" to Mosby's command. Harney was briefly held in the Alexandria jail, then transferred to the Old Capitol prison in Washington. He disappeared into the prisoner of war system and was never heard from again.

Confederate records put a different slant on Harney's mission. He was one of two "operators" assigned to the Torpedo Bureau in Richmond, the organization responsible for using explosive devices against the Union. The rest of the bureau's operators were assigned to the field.

The next piece of the story can be found in the memoirs of Brigadier General Edward Hastings Ripley. Ripley, commanding a brigade of Vermont troops, was briefly the senior Union officer occupying Richmond when the Confederate capital fell on April 3, 1865.

According to Ripley, after President Lincoln had toured the captured city on foot, a Confederate soldier, William H. Snyder, came to his head-quarters and begged for an interview. Snyder told Ripley that he was assigned to the Torpedo Bureau and that a few days earlier a party had left the bureau with a mission, "which vaguely he understood was aimed at the head of the Yankee government." Snyder could give no further details because the Torpedo Bureau's operations were compartmented so that nobody knew the particulars of another's assignment. Ripley did get a lot of additional information from Snyder that confirmed his knowledge of Confederate clandestine activity. But when Ripley tried to get Lincoln to hear Snyder's story, the president refused.

Confederate records show that Snyder had been assigned to the Torpedo Bureau two months earlier and thus would have been personally familiar with some of its activities. The only mission he could have had in mind was the one on which Harney had been sent.

Based on the date of Harney's capture and Snyder's report of his departure, Harney must have left Richmond on or about April 1. On that date the Confederates in Richmond did not know that they would have to begin evacuating the city the following day. Also on that date, the Treasury issued a warrant for $1,500 in gold from the account labeled "secret service," to be given to Judah Benjamin. Money from this account was used for action projects, not espionage. Although Benjamin already had access to $1,500 in gold, it was money approved for other purposes and not approved for the type of action that the secret service account was intended to cover. There is no request voucher for $1,500 on record in the Library of Congress, but the actual warrant has survived. The request, signed by Jefferson Davis, was probably lost in the confusion of the city's evacuation before it could be recorded.

Harney's mission could only have involved a target of great importance. He was one of the few practitioners of a rare technology — the art of explosives. Colonel Mosby made a substantial effort to escort Harney despite having earlier received orders to move his command to the west of Orange, Virginia. One of Mosby's men later described Harney's loss as "irretrievable." The only target that could have been important enough to merit such priority of effort was the White House.

Jefferson Davis, president of the Confederacy, personally controlled the money used for secret service operations.

This surmise is confirmed by the report of an interrogation of George Atzerodt, one of Booth's associates. In the interrogation Atzerodt said mining the White House was one of the projects under consideration. Further substantiation can be found in the developing military situation of the time. Grant's army was pressing Richmond on one side while Sherman's troops were approaching from the other. The Confederates were planning to evacuate Richmond and combine the armies of Lee and Johnston with the intention of defeating Sherman. The feeling was that such a defeat would cause the war-weary North to agree to peace. The only coordination between Grant and Sherman was through Washington; if the command in Washington could be disrupted, Confederate success might be guaranteed.

Booth apparently decided to shoot Lincoln only a day or two before he carried out the assassination. This would have been after it became obvious that Harney was not present to help create an explosion. Booth's choice of targets reflected those men that the Confederacy must have hoped would have been killed in an explosion at the White House during a meeting of cabinet officials. According to the law in effect then, if the president and vice president were both incapacitated, the secretary of state was required to call for a meeting of electors the following December for the purpose of electing a new president. Booth's target list, therefore, included President Lincoln, Vice President Andrew Johnson, and Secretary of State William Seward. In their absence, there would have been chaos in Washington.

Colonel John S. Mosby.

As it turned out, Booth was the only one to get his target. The man assigned to kill Johnson had no enthusiasm for his assignment and got drunk instead. The man assigned to kill Seward injured him severely but not mortally. Additionally, Secretary of War Edwin Stanton may have been targeted; he was convinced that a broken doorbell had saved him from assassination.

One can surmise that Booth was distressed at his failure to capture Lincoln and anxious to show his Confederate colleagues that he was capable of decisive action. Furthermore, he did not know the true military situation and apparently acted without consulting anybody who did. Lee had surrendered the Army of Northern Virginia on April 9, 1865, just five days before the assassination. In retrospect, that date marks the end of the Civil War, but at the time this was not so apparent. There were still Rebel forces in the field, and so few soldiers had surrendered with Lee that many people thought that the majority of his army had escaped. Booth apparently thought he could still influence the outcome of the war by his actions. Somebody more in touch with military reality would probably have understood that the Confederacy was beyond saving.

In summary, conventional explanations of the assassination were formed before the facts just described had been identified. Contrary to popular belief, the Confederates had an active secret service adept at the use of explosives. It's true that there is no list of clandestine agents with John Wilkes Booth's name on it, but there is ample evidence that he acted like one and therefore probably was one. There is a good deal of evidence pointing to a failed plot to kidnap Lincoln. Furthermore, the Confederates had every reason in 1865 to target the Union high command. It's my contention that the actions taken by Booth clearly were an attempt to approximate the damage that would have been caused by an explosion in the White House.

Brigadier General William A. Tidwell has served in the U.S. intelligence community since World War II, including twenty-three years with the Central Intelligence Agency. He is co-author of Come Retribution: The Confederate Secret Service and the Assassination of Lincoln *and author of* April '65: Confederate Covert Action in the American Civil War.

April 14, 1865: The assassin at center stage.

3

An April Tragedy

A BRAHAM LINCOLN DIDN'T BELIEVE IN DREAMS or visions, or at least not nearly to the extent that his wife (despite her denials) did. But according to the reminiscences of Ward Hill Lamon, a strapping family friend from Illinois and the president's self-appointed bodyguard, there was one particular nightmare that the president couldn't let go of.

One evening, about the time that Booth's kidnaping plot was unraveling, the Lincolns went to see *Faust*. The performance inspired a dark dream in Lincoln. A few nights later, he shared it with friends during an intimate gathering inside the White House.

"About ten days ago," he began, "I retired very late. I had been waiting up for important dispatches. I could not have been very long in bed when I fell into a slumber, for I was weary. I soon began to dream. There seemed to be a death-like stillness around me. Then I heard subdued sobs, as if a number of people were weeping. I thought I left my bed and wandered downstairs.

"There the silence was broken by the same pitiful sobbing, but the mourners were invisible. I went from room to room. No living person was in sight, but the same mournful sounds of distress met me as I passed along. It was light in all of the rooms; every object was familiar to me, but where were all the people who were grieving as if their hearts would break?

"I was puzzled and alarmed. What could be the meaning of all this? Determined to find the cause of a state of things so mysterious and so shocking, I kept on until I arrived in the East Room, which I entered. There I met

General Ulysses S. Grant, with wife and son, at winter quarters in City Point in early 1865. It had been announced that the Grants would join the Lincolns at the theater on the evening of April 14, but the general's wife, remembering a previous run-in with Mary Lincoln, was able to wiggle out of the invitation.

with a sickening surprise. Before me was a catafalque, on which rested a corpse in funeral vestments. Around it were stationed soldiers who were acting as guards; and there was a throng of people, some gazing mournfully upon the corpse, whose face was covered, others weeping pitifully.

"'Who is dead in the White House?' I demanded of one of the soldiers.

"'The president,' was his answer. 'He was killed by an assassin.'

"Then came a loud burst of grief from the crowd, which awoke me from my dream. I slept no more that night, and although it was only a dream, I have been strangely annoyed by it ever since."

The room was silent. Guests accustomed to Lincoln's humor didn't know what to say about this premonition of death.

"This is horrid," said Mary Lincoln. She was clearly frightened by what she had just heard. "I wish you had not told it. I am glad I don't believe in dreams, or I should be in terror from this time forth."

Over the years Mary Todd Lincoln has been incorrectly pictured as wearing this evening gown and wreath of flowers on the night of the assassination. But observers remembered her wearing a dark bonnet and light gray, silk spring dress.

Lincoln sought to calm her. "It was only a dream, Mother. Let us say no more about it, and try to forget it."

This famous episode, so integral a part of Lincoln lore, was first recounted in an 1895 book by Lamon. However, according to Richard Sloan, a modern researcher who has studied Lincoln's portrayal in the performing arts, Lamon's dream story is very similar to one that appeared in the first play produced about the assassination. The only difference is that, in the 1867 stage version, an angel has the dream. Could it be that the play supplied material for Lamon's reminiscences?

Even if it did, there is no doubt that the possibility of personal harm weighed heavily on Lincoln's mind as the war wound down. In the late afternoon of April 14, 1865, he and a guard, William Crook, walked to the War Department. Despite all of the recent good news, the president seemed despondent.

"Crook, do you know, I believe there are men who want to take my life." Dropping his voice, he added: "And I have no doubt they will do it."

"Why do you think so, Mr. President?" asked Crook.

"Other men have been assassinated," he replied. "I know no one could do it and escape alive. But it is to be done, it is impossible to prevent it."

Crook thought it odd when, a few hours later, as the Lincolns left for Ford's Theater in their carriage, the president said, "Good-bye, Crook," instead of "Good night." It was as if he didn't plan on coming back.

★

Nobody knows exactly when Booth's intentions turned bloody. There may have been no grand epiphany, simply a growing realization that kidnaping had become too impractical, or, given the Confederacy's rapidly deteriorating military situation, that a much more radical act was needed if there was to be any chance of saving the South. At least through the end of March 1865, it appears that Booth still intended to capture the president. However, the focus of the attempt had shifted to Ford's Theater. According to a newspaper item Booth read on March 27, the Lincolns had bought tickets for several upcoming plays there.

On March 23, five days after the bungled kidnaping attempt, Lincoln embarked on the longest journey of his presidency, a seventeen-day tour of the front that coincided with the Confederacy's final collapse. With Lincoln out of the city for an indeterminate time, Booth and his associates went their separate ways. Arnold and O'Laughlen (who Booth owed $500) had grown disenchanted with the abduction plot; the others waited a call to action.

Booth spent the first week of April in Boston, the city where he had performed most often during his career. Whether he was there to confer with Confederate agents, borrow money, or both, remains a mystery. During his stay, Petersburg and then Richmond fell. On Palm Sunday, April 9, General Lee surrendered the 22,000-man Army of Northern Virginia to Grant at Appomattox Courthouse. Word reached Lincoln as he was returning by steamship to Washington, gaily reciting long passages from *Macbeth*. Although Jefferson Davis and his cabinet had safely fled Richmond and large, scattered units of Confederate soldiers were still in the field, the outcome of four years of bloody rebellion was no longer in doubt. In the North, at least, people thought that it was all over except for the shouting.

In Boston, Booth may have read the report of a *Boston Journal* correspondent who witnessed Lincoln's remarkable entrance into Richmond on April 3. The fallen capital's white citizens had shrunk behind doors and windows, but the Negro population turned out in force. An old black woman, said the reporter, squinted uncertainly at the tall, rumpled figure slowly walking through the devastated streets and then, recognizing him as the Great Emancipator, "jumped straight up and down, shouting, 'Glory, glory, glory,' till her voice was lost in the universal cheer." Soldiers had to force a wedge through the delirious throngs of ex-slaves. Upon reaching the stone mansion that had served as the Confederate White House, Lincoln was shown Jefferson Davis's armchair. He sank wearily into it and asked for a glass of water.

Lincoln's impertinent rest stop galled Booth. A few years earlier, when John Sleeper Clarke had made some flippant remark about the president of the Confederacy, he had become unglued, grabbing his brother-in-law by the throat and hissing,

An interior view of Ford's Theater in 1865.

"Never, if you value your life, never speak in that way to me again of a man and a cause I hold sacred."

Now, back in Washington—a city suddenly alive with fireworks, cannonades, drunken toasts, and torchlit revelry—the imagery continued to offend. "Why, that old scoundrel, Lincoln," he growled to his actor friend, Edwin Emerson. "He went into Jeff Davis' house in Richmond, sat down and threw his long legs over the arm of a chair and squirted tobacco juice all over the place. Somebody ought to kill him." For emphasis he broke Emerson's cane into pieces.

Booth's past bonhomie and temperance had given way to easy irritability and bouts of heavy drinking. He was broke and had been made to look like a fool. While all around him people celebrated by hanging Jeff Davis in effigy and gathering in front of the White House to serenade the president, he struggled to keep depression at bay. A friend offered to buy him a drink. "Yes," Booth said, "anything to drive away the blues."

Those still taken in by Booth's celebrity and patriotic ardor maintained their faith in him. Mary Surratt kept a photograph of the handsome actor tucked away behind a picture on the wall and Powell respectfully addressed his social and intellectual superior as "Captain." Others still responded to his orders. Per Booth's instructions, Edman Spangler sold the wagon he had been caretaking for him in the alley behind Ford's Theater, while Atzerodt tried to find buyers for Booth's horses. On the surface, this clearance sale was nothing more than a quick way to raise cash. However, with the horses and wagon gone, there was no ready way to transport a captive. And Booth now had Powell scouting the house of Secretary of State William H. Seward, who was confined to his bed because of a broken jaw suffered in a recent carriage accident. Obviously there had been some change in plans, though Booth chose not to share it with the others. Maybe he hadn't finalized it in his own mind.

On the evening of Tuesday, April 11, several of the conspirators listened to Lincoln speak to a large, jubilant crowd from a second-story window of the executive mansion. The speech dealt principally with the upcoming problems of reconstruction. When Lincoln spoke of limited black suffrage, the offended Booth told Powell to pull out his pistol and shoot the president right then and there. When Powell declined, he spit out to Arnold, "That means nigger citizenship. Now, by God, I'll put him through."

Walking away, Booth added: "That is the last speech he will ever make." He was right.

★

April 14, 1865, was a warm, radiant Good Friday, alive with the perfume of lilac and the prospect of peace. That morning Booth went to the barbershop for a shave and a haircut, accompanied by Powell, O'Laughlen, and Herold. Meanwhile, Booth had Atzerodt check into the Kirkwood House, where Vice President Andrew Johnson was staying. Booth then strolled over to Grover's Theater on Pennsylvania Avenue to idly inquire about the Lincolns' anticipated attendance at that evening's performance of *Aladdin.* He was told that the president and his wife would not be coming.

The Good Friday performance of Our American Cousin *was billed as a benefit for Laura Keene. The 39-year-old actress was appearing for the final time in her role as Florence Trenchard.*

Stopping at Ford's Theater to pick up his mail, Booth learned from his old friend, proprietor H. Clay "Harry" Ford, that the Lincolns would be coming there that night. The occasion was the benefit and farewell of actress Laura Keene in the popular comedy, *Our American Cousin.* The theater had already placed notices in both afternoon dailies, apprising the public that the president and wife would be accompanied by General and Mrs. Grant. "Unconditional Surrender" Grant was the man of the hour and his presence was sure to guarantee a packed house.

Lincoln's box as it looked on the evening of the assassination.

Booth moved quickly. He'd always enjoyed free access to the theater, and that afternoon he took full advantage of the privilege. He was in and out several times, moseying around the "state box" that was hurriedly being decorated with some borrowed flags and bunting and a framed portrait of George Washington. He also rode his rented horse in circles several times in the alley, perfecting his getaway. He stopped in at the adjacent Star Saloon to have several drinks with the stagehands. He seemed in a "happy frame of mind," remembered a teenaged orderly who turned down Booth's offer of a drink, but did accept a free cigar.

In mid-afternoon, Booth went to Surratt's boardinghouse. The day after the kidnaping attempt, John Surratt had hidden Booth's carbines in the floorboards above the kitchen inside Surratt's Tavern, a potentially incriminating stash that worried

John M. Lloyd, the tenant. John now was out of town, having been dispatched by the Confederate government to Elmira, New York, to report on prisoners being held there. Booth asked Mrs. Surratt if she would take a pair of field glasses out to her tavern, to add to his secret arsenal of guns and equipment.

At around 3:30 Booth visited the Kirkwood House to leave a short note for the vice president. "Don't wish to disturb you," it said. "Are you at home? J. Wilkes Booth." The idea was to throw suspicion on Johnson. Since he would automatically accede to the presidency upon Lincoln's death, the note could be interpreted as meaning the vice president was in cahoots with the conspirators. When Booth returned to Ford's Theater, he ran into John Mathews, an actor friend. He handed Mathews a sealed envelope. Inside was a letter to the *National Intelligencer*, which he asked Mathews to deliver the following day for publication. In the midst of the commotion that was to occur a few hours later, Mathews forgot about Booth's letter. It would be Saturday night before the distraught Mathews, suddenly remembering what had been given him, tore open the envelope. The letter, whose existence the frightened actor kept secret for two years lest he be implicated in the assassination, chilled him:

> When Caesar had conquered the enemies of Rome and the power that was his menaced the liberties of the people, Brutus arose and slew him. The stroke of his dagger was guided by his love for Rome. It was the spirit and ambition of Caesar that Brutus struck at.
>
> 'O then that we could come by Caesar's spirit, And not dismember Caesar! But Alas! Caesar must bleed for it!'
> I answer with Brutus.

*

The president began the last full day of his life at 7 A.M. The morning was devoted to paperwork, interviews, and a visit to the War Department. At 11 o'clock the cabinet met, with Grant present. Talk involved reconstruction, and Lincoln allowed as to how he wanted no part of trying and hanging Confederate high officials. "Frighten them out of the country," he said, flapping his long arms. "Open the gates, let down the bars, scare them off—shoo!" A minute or two later he added: "We must extinguish our resentments if we expect harmony and union."

Grant stayed for a personal chat with the president, informing him of his regrets in having to miss that evening's show. He and Mrs. Grant were anxious to rejoin their children in New Jersey as soon as possible.

The fatal shot, as depicted in Leslie's Illustrated Newspaper *(top), and the assassin's leap to the stage, as sketched by a* Harper's Weekly *artist.*

The president understood—too well. He knew that Mary Lincoln had been rude to Mrs. Grant on several previous occasions. The last thing the general's wife wanted was to spend an evening in close quarters with that irrational woman.

After Grant left, Lincoln occupied himself with more paperwork. He signed the pardon of a deserter with the observation, "Well, I think the boy can do us more good above ground than under," and ordered the release of a Confederate spy sentenced to die. He had dinner and then dressed for the theater, once again tucking the white formal gloves Mary Lincoln was always badgering him to wear into his pocket.

The Lincolns found it surprisingly hard to find a couple to accompany them. Several people had been invited and all had offered various excuses. Finally, a pair was found: Miss Clara

The derringer Booth used to fire the fatal shot into the back of the president's head was a compact weapon, just six inches long and weighing only eight ounces. It is now on display at the Ford's Theater National Historic Site.

Harris, the sweet-faced, full-figured daughter of Senator Ira T. Harris of New York, escorted by her twenty-eight-year-old fiance, the tall and quiet Major Henry Rathbone. After saying good-bye to his worried guard, William Crook, and the equally concerned Secretary of War Stanton, the president joined Mrs. Lincoln in their carriage. On the way they stopped to pick up the young couple at the senator's home on H Street, near Fourteenth, then continued on to Ford's Theater in good spirits.

At about the same time that the presidential party was en route to the theater, Booth was huddled with what was left of his action team inside Lewis Powell's room at the Herndon House, a block from the theater. Present was Booth, Powell, Atzerodt, and Herold. O'Laughlen had begged off to go drinking with some friends from Baltimore. Atzerodt and Powell would both later claim that this was the very first time—at 8 o'clock on the evening of April 14—that Booth talked of assassinating the president. And not only the president, as Booth went on to explain, but also General Grant, who he would murder alongside Lincoln, Secretary of State Seward—to be taken out by Powell—and Vice President Johnson, to be eliminated by Atzerodt. The attacks were to occur simultaneously, with the assassins in position to strike their respective targets beginning at 10 o'clock. Herold, who knew Washington and surrounding environs like the back of his tiny, soft hands, would put his only known asset to use, accompanying Powell to Seward's house and, after the attack, guiding him out of the city. They would meet up at or beyond the Navy Yard Bridge, the quickest route out of Washington, pick up their carbines and supplies at Surratt's tavern, and, with the help of established contacts in southern Maryland, cross over into Virginia and continue to head south.

Atzerodt was shaken by this sudden change in plans. He'd signed on for a kidnaping, not murder. Booth probably wasn't too surprised by his reaction, having left the note in Johnson's box to allow for the possibility that the easy-going German would fail in his mission.

Why now, with the South all but finished, did Booth outline an attack that targeted not one, but four, high officials? Opportunity and revenge come immediately to mind. Lincoln and Grant—who Booth expected to be in the box—were in his opinion the two men most responsible for waging the total war that had brought so much suffering and hardship to the South. To think that they could be taken out in one fell swoop! Having accomplished this twin killing, why not go after others judged equally at fault? Seward and Johnson were obvious and convenient targets who could be murdered in their rooms and whose deaths would throw the government and the issue of presidential succession into turmoil. Meanwhile, the South could take advantage of the confusion and regain the upper hand in a war that Booth, Powell, the Surratts, and thousands like them had yet to declare over in their minds. The brandy Booth had been imbibing for weeks had to have played a part in this addled thinking; little else explains his faith in such unremarkable and unproven characters as Atzerodt and Herold.

Setting aside the logistical and tactical advantages of staging his assault inside familiar Ford's Theater, Booth chose the site for maximum dramatic impact. Let Atzerodt and Powell do their bloody deeds inside an empty bed chamber. His primary concern was that of all egotists: Why do something if nobody's watching?

⋆

It was about 8:30 P.M. when the presidential party arrived at Ford's Theater. The first act had started, but upon the president's entrance the play stopped, the crowd rose to its feet, and the orchestra struck up *Hail to the Chief*. John Downing was among many theatergoers disappointed to find an ordinary major substituting for the heroic General Grant.

"We soon got over our disappointment however," Downing later wrote a friend, "observing the play. . . . The acting was excellent as of course, it would be with Laura Keene's company—and the President and Mrs. Lincoln seemed to enjoy it highly—the latter, in particular laughing often and very heartily. I could detect a broad smile on Uncle Abraham's face very often, while, at other times, he rested his face in both of his hands, bending forward, and seemingly buried in deep thought."

Management had carefully furnished and decorated the presidential box, which was made more spacious by removing a partition and combining boxes seven and eight. The boxes, which stood about ten feet high (level to the first balcony) and to the actors' left (the audience's right), actually were comparatively poor ones for watching a play. But sightlines had been judged of secondary importance when the theater was built two years earlier. The owners were more concerned about filling these luxury suites with people who wanted to be seen. Thus many of the people in the audience had a good view of the occupants and their seating arrangements. Miss Harris was seated in one of two stuffed chairs, in front of Major Rathbone, who lounged on the sofa placed against the back of the box. Mrs. Lincoln was seated in the other stuffed chair, next to her husband, who sank with satisfaction into a comfortable Victorian rocking chair,

Actor William Ferguson was backstage when tragedy struck. The fleeing Booth passed so closely to the stunned Ferguson "that I felt his breath upon my face."

upholstered in red satin, that the Fords had brought out of storage.

Less thought was given to guarding the occupants. Remarkably, no can say with certainty who was charged with Lincoln's protection that night. John F. Parker, a private police-

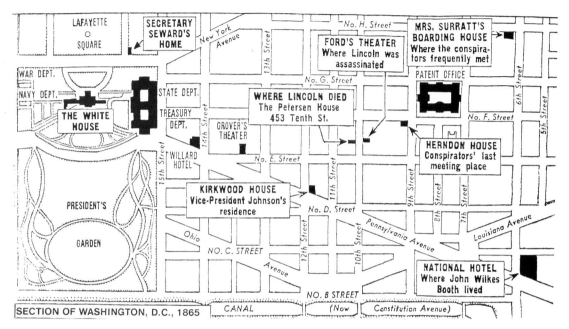

The area of major activity in Washington on April 14, 1865.

man with a history of drunkenness and dereliction of duty, is most often thought have been given the assignment; indeed, he was later charged with abandoning his post in favor of a quick drink at a nearby tavern (and acquitted). The capable Ward Hill Lamon would ordinarily have served as a bodyguard, but to his eternal regret he was in Richmond on assignment. After all of these years, the mystery will probably never be resolved. But somebody took a chair outside the presidential box that night and let Booth, on the strength of his familiar face and a calling card, enter.

It was sometime around 10:15, with the third act in progress. Booth had been in and out of the theater several times while the play was in progress, leaving to fortify himself with a stiff drink of whiskey before returning. In the alley, Edman Spangler was supposed to be holding the reins of his mare. Now, Booth's frenzied preparations earlier in the day were about to pay off. That afternoon, while the theater was empty, he had bored a finger-sized peephole in the inner door to the box. This gave him a perfect view of the back of Lincoln's rocking chair. He'd also gouged a mortise in the plaster wall opposite the door leading into the corridor. By bracing a wooden bar between the door and the wall, he was able to prevent anyone from rushing through the jammed door. From under his coat he pulled a .44-caliber derringer pistol and a nine-inch knife.

Mary Lincoln would give two different accounts of her husband's last words. At first, she remembered that she had been leaning close to him, her hand on his knobby knee, and said playfully, "What will Miss Harris think of my hanging on to you so?" To which Lincoln replied: "She won't think anything about it."

Secretary of State William H. Seward was recuperating from an accident inside his Lafayette Square residence when he was attacked.

Her other version had the president, perhaps waking from some private daydream, improbably saying, "How I should like to visit Jerusalem sometime!"

In the play, comic lead Harry Hawk played Asa Trenchard, an American backwoodsman trying to pass himself off as a millionaire. Hawk was alone on the stage when he responded to the gold-digging mother who had just discovered he was as poor as a church mouse. "Don't know the manners of good society, eh?" he said. "Well, I guess I know enough to turn you inside out, old gal—you sockdologizing old mantrap!"

Frederick Seward's Encounter with the Assassin.

Lewis Powell pistol-whipped Frederick Seward at the start of a violent assault that left five badly slashed and beaten victims in its wake. No assassin in U.S. history had ever injured as many people in a single attack.

Hawk was looking in Mrs. Lincoln's direction as he delivered the lines. He would always remember that she was smiling at the very moment a shot rang out in the president's box.

★

Long seconds of quiet bewilderment were followed by outright pandemonium. Edwin Emerson was standing in the wings, waiting for his cue to go on, when he heard the *cra-a-ck*! of a pistol. He described the delayed reaction and ensuing chaos:

I was not surprised, nor was anyone else behind the scenes. Such sounds are too common during the shifting of the various sets to surprise an actor. For a good many seconds after that sound nothing happened behind the footlights. Then, as I stood there in the dimness, a man rushed by me, making for the stage door. I did not recognize Booth at the time, nor did anyone else, I think, unless perhaps someone out on the stage, when he stood a moment and shouted with theatrical gesture, *"Sic Semper Tyrannis*! (So perish all tyrants!)" Even after he flashed by, there was quiet for a few moments among the actors and the stage hands. No one knew what had happened.

Then the fearful cry, springing from nowhere it seemed, ran like wildfire behind the scenes:

"The President's shot!"

Everyone began to swirl hither and thither in hysterical aimlessness. Still the curtain had not been rung down—for no one seemed to have retained a scintilla of self-possession—and the actors on the stage were left standing there as though paralyzed.

Then someone dropped the curtain and pandemonium commenced. The police came rushing in to add to the chaos, and for what seemed an hour, the confusion was indescribable. One incident stands out plainly in my memory from the confusion of men and sound that turned the stage into chaos. As I was running aimlessly to and fro behind the scenes—as everyone else was—a young lady, coming out from a dressing room, asked the cause of all the uproar.

"President Lincoln has just been shot!" I replied.

"Oh!" she exclaimed and, closing her eyes, was sinking limp to the floor in a faint when I caught her and carried her into her dressing room. She was Miss Jennie Gourlay, one of the then well-known family of actors, and that night playing the part of Mary Trenchard.

Sergeant George F. Robinson. In 1871, the soldier-nurse was awarded a special medal from Congress for his role in saving Secretary Seward's life.

Andrew Johnson was a self-taught former tailor who climbed the political ladder to become military governor of Tennessee, vice president and, upon Lincoln's death, the seventeenth president of the United States. Johnson was variously described as a drunk and a demagogue by those close to Lincoln. He also was a survivor, emerging unscathed during the bloodletting of April 14 and, by a single vote, avoiding impeachment during his only term in the White House.

"Booth, being an actor, was familiar with the stage," actress Katherine Evans, who was inside the dressing room with Gourlay, told the *New York Tribune* years later:

He ran between Hawk and Billy Ferguson, struck at [William] Withers, our orchestra leader, with his knife, and made his way out through the stage door into the alley where "Peanut Johnnie" the boy who sold peanuts in the gallery was holding his horse.

I looked and saw President Lincoln unconscious, his head dropping on his breast, his eyes closed, but with a smile still on his face. Mrs. Lincoln had risen from her seat beside him and was stroking his cheeks. . . .

In an instant the theater was in an uproar. It was crowded to the top-most gallery, and every one had risen in his seat. Men were shouting and climbing out into the aisles. Miss Keene was making her way up to where the president lay wounded, and several doctors from the audience were trying to force a passage through the crowd. Dr. Charles Taft was lifted up into the box from the stage, while many persons, some of them physicians, were crowding into the narrow aisle which led into the box and were pounding on the door, demanding admission.

The report of the derringer "seemed to proceed from behind the President's box," remembered Dr. Taft, who was enjoying the play from his front row seat:

The dying president is carried across the street to the house of William Petersen, a German tailor.

MURDER OF PRESIDENT LINCOLN – MR. LINCOLN CARRIED FROM THE THEATRE TO PETERSEN'S HOUSE, OPPOSITE, APRIL 14.

While it startled everyone in the audience, it was evidently
accepted by all as an introductory effect preceding some new
situation in the play, several of which had been introduced in
the earlier part of the performance. A moment afterward a hatless and white-faced man leaped from the front of the
president's box down twelve feet to the stage. As he jumped,
one of the spurs on his riding boots caught in the folds of the
flag dropped over the front, and caused him to fall partly on his
hands and knees as he struck the stage. Springing quickly to his
feet with the suppleness of an athlete, he faced the audience for
a moment as he brandished in his right hand a long knife, and
shouted *"Sic Semper Tyrannis!"* Then, with a rapid stage stride,
he crossed the stage, and disappeared from view. A piercing
shriek from the president's box, a repeated call for "Water!
water!" and "A surgeon!" in quick succession, conveyed the
truth to the almost paralyzed audience. A most terrible scene
of excitement followed. With loud shouts of "Kill him!"

*The first doctor to Lincoln's side was
Charles Augustus Leale, who had
only recently graduated from medical
school.*

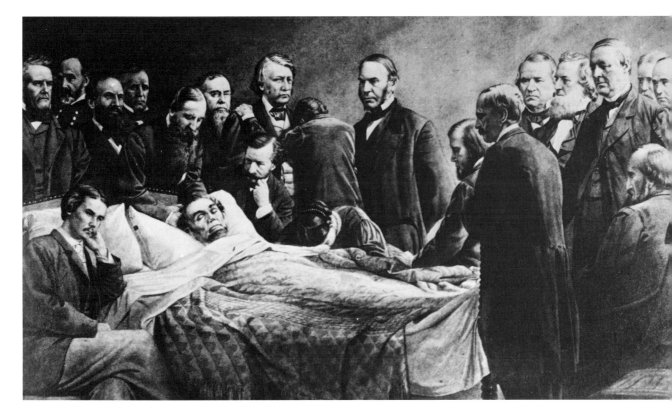

*Practically every print made of Lincoln's death is inaccurate in the identification, number, and positioning of the mourners
present. At least one image is correct in this tableau created by Alexander Gardner: the president's son, Robert (center),
weeping on the shoulder of Charles Sumner.*

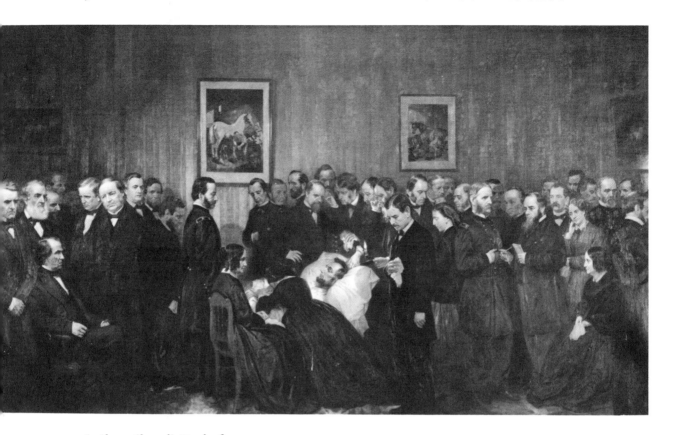

In Alonzo Chappel's Death of Lincoln, *the ten-by-fifteen-foot bedroom has been expanded into a huge chamber, the only way the artist could squeeze forty-six people into the scene.*

"Lynch him!" part of the audience stampeded towards the entrance and some to the stage.

I leaped from the top of the orchestra railing in front of me upon the stage, and, announcing myself as an army surgeon, was immediately lifted up to the president's box by several gentlemen who had collected beneath. . . .

When I entered the box, the president was lying upon the floor surrounded by his wailing wife and several gentlemen who had entered from the private stairway and dress circle. Assistant Surgeon Charles A. Leale . . . had caused the coat and waistcoat to be cut off in searching for the wound. Dr. A.F.A. King of Washington was also present, and assisted in the examination. The carriage had been ordered to remove the president to the White House, but the surgeons countermanded the order, and he was removed to a bed in the house opposite the theater. . . .

All in all, the assassination had gone smoothly. Booth had quietly opened the inner door of the box, crept up behind the president's chair, and fired his derringer at point-blank range at the left side of Lincoln's head. The ball crashed through his skull behind the left ear, then tunneled its way diagonally across the brain before stopping behind his right eye. Lincoln's head slumped forward, his whiskered chin resting on his chest. He never regained consciousness.

Before anybody in the box could really react, Booth had pushed his way between the president and Mrs. Lincoln. Major Rathbone, confused, jumped off the sofa and began grappling with the dark-clothed assailant. Booth slashed at Rathbone with his knife, a blow the officer parried with his left arm. The blade inflicted a terrible wound, slicing the officer's arm all the way to the bone. Booth then jumped from the box onto the stage, a leap he had made many times as an actor, stopping just long enough to make a declaration. There is no agreement as to Booth's exact words—a cruel irony for a seasoned thespian who had undoubtedly chosen his parting lines with great care and with an eye to history. After his utterance, the nineteenth-century Brutus in knee-high riding boots and spurs darted into the night, leaving behind a gas-lit cauldron of confusion.

At about the same time that Booth was leveling his derringer at the back of Lincoln's head, Lewis Powell was single-handedly turning the secretary of state's house on Lafayette Park, just across from the White House, into a war zone. Having talked his way past a servant and through the front door with the story that he was delivering medicine for Seward, he was met with skepticism by the secretary's son, Frederick. Agreeing to leave, Powell suddenly pulled out a revolver and fired. When it failed to go off, he crashed it down on Frederick's head, shattering his skull and the pistol.

Pulling out a large Bowie knife, Powell rushed up the stairs to Seward's bedroom. Fanny Seward, the secretary's fragile twenty-one-year-old daughter, was knocked unconscious with a single powerful blow. An army nurse, Sergeant George Robinson, was thrown aside before Powell jumped on the secretary's bed. In the dimly lit room Powell thrust again and again into Seward's face, looking to slash his jugular. Luckily for Seward, he was wearing a brace that deflected several of the blows. Robinson and another of Seward's sons, Major Augustus Seward, pulled Powell off. In the ensuing struggle, Augustus

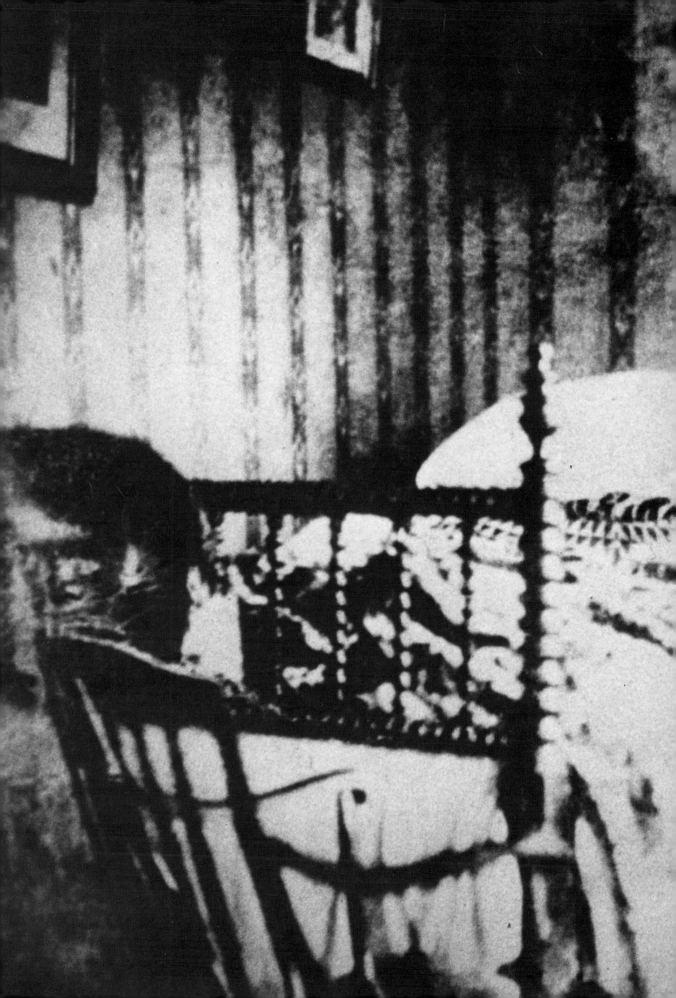

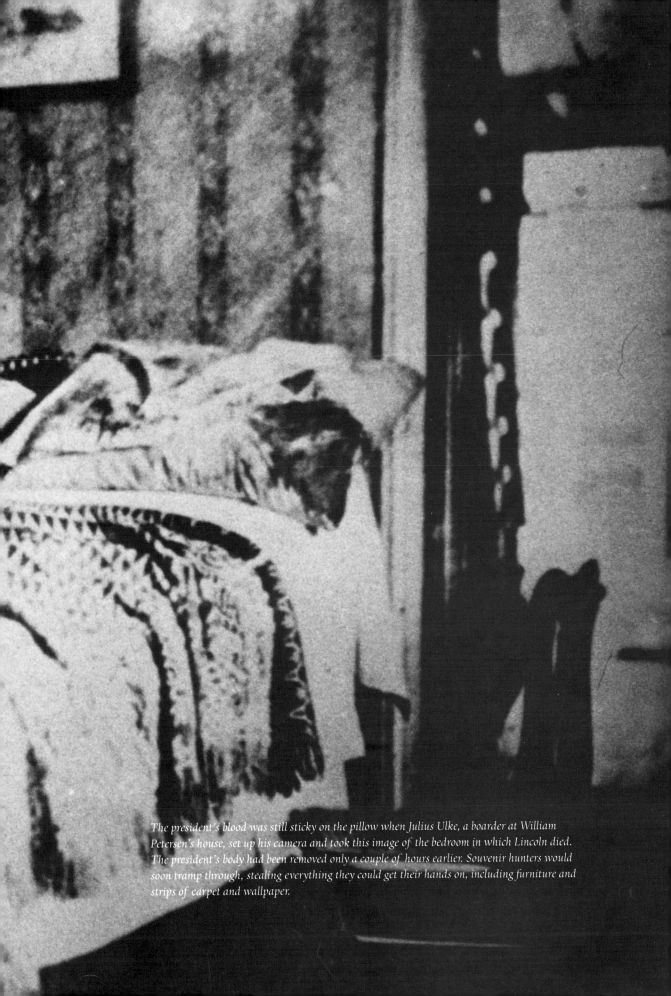

The president's blood was still sticky on the pillow when Julius Ulke, a boarder at William Petersen's house, set up his camera and took this image of the bedroom in which Lincoln died. The president's body had been removed only a couple of hours earlier. Souvenir hunters would soon tramp through, stealing everything they could get their hands on, including furniture and strips of carpet and wallpaper.

was stabbed seven times and Robinson four. The assailant ran out the front door shouting, "I'm mad! I'm mad!" On his way out he plunged his knife into the chest of Emerick Hansell, a messenger who had innocently stumbled onto the carnage.

Powell had been a one-man wrecking crew, leaving five badly slashed and beaten victims in his wake. All would sur-

Ford Theater, draped in black following the assassination.

vive, though the secretary would carry horrible scars on his face for the rest of his life and his daughter would never fully recover from the trauma, passing away the following year.

But the warrior found himself unexpectedly alone. Where was his escort, Herold?

Herold, who had galloped off to check on the attack on the vice president, was asking the same question about Atzerodt. He wasn't at the Kirkwood House. Herold, not really giving a damn about anything at this point except his own safety, spurred his stolen horse on through the streets of Washington, towards the Navy Yard Bridge.

And where was Atzerodt? The would-be assassin spent this night of mayhem and murder in a local tavern, getting drunk.

★

Dr. Charles A. Leale, only two months out of medical school, was the first doctor to reach Lincoln. "Oh, doctor," cried Mary

Lincoln, "do what you can for my dear husband! Is he dead? Can he recover?" Leale spotted the clot behind the left ear. He removed it, then dug his finger into the opening. Blood flowed and the breathing became more regular.

Leale was quickly joined by more physicians. It was clear that there was nothing much that could be done for the president. He was paralyzed and his pulse was weak. "His wound is mortal," said Leale. "It is impossible for him to recover."

The decision was made to take the president to the nearest bed. Across the street, a young boarder directed that he be brought into the house of William Petersen, a German tailor who was his landlord. With blood and brain matter seeping out his wound and half of his clothes cut off, the once vital figure of Abraham Lincoln was carried into a small bedroom at the end of the first-floor hallway. It turned out that his six-foot, four-inch frame was too long for the bed. Unable to break the footboard off, Dr. Leale directed that his body be placed diagonally across the mattress. That is how Lincoln spent the last nine hours of his life, his large, bare feet sticking out by the wall, his swelling, discolored, bleeding head propped up on two large pillows.

Charles Sumner, the abolitionist senator from Massachusetts, hurried to the Petersen House with the president's oldest son, Robert. Sumner took the president's hand in his.

"It's no use," one of the doctors said. "He can't hear you. He is dead."

"No, he isn't dead," insisted Sumner desperately. "Look at his face, he's breathing."

"It will never be anything more than this," the doctor said.

Robert Lincoln wept and Sumner put his arm around him, waiting, like all the rest, for the end to finally come. Outside it was raining. Upwards of ninety different people made their way into the cramped bedroom at one time or another. These included sixteen doctors who were frantic to try anything— mustard plasters, hot water bottles, blankets—to keep him warm and his great heart beating, and a hysterical Mary Lincoln, whose shrieking finally got her removed for good at three in the morning. At times the only sounds were the raindrops tapping the windowpane and the ominous ticking of the clock. The passing seconds boomed like artillery inside the still room. There was nothing to do but to wait and pray. Dr. Leale kept the president's hand in his throughout, "so that in the darkness he would know he had a friend," he explained.

Finally, at 7:22 A.M., Lincoln slipped away.

"He belongs to the angels now," said Edwin Stanton, tears streaming into his beard. That is how the attendant stenographer, James Tanner, remembered his words. Those not quite satisfied with their dramatic impact, however, would soon amend the secretary of war's epitaph to, "Now he belongs to the ages." Which is how history chooses to remember it.

That sad, rainy Saturday, in another part of the city, Edwin Bates sat down to write a letter to his parents. He had been sitting up front at orchestra level when the shot was fired. He identified the cause of so much sorrow.

"His name is John Wilkes Booth," Bates informed them, "an actor & who has frequently played in this theater & conversant with the different places of egress from it. He had not until last night ever succeeded in attaining any reputation in his profession as an actor but now he has acquired a reputation in tragedy which will render him famous & infamous in history in all time."

Sarah Bush Lincoln, born in 1788, outlived her famous stepson by four years. When a relative came by her cabin on the Illinois prairie to tell her of the assassination, she replied, "I knowed they'd kill him. I been awaiting for it."

Two Who Were There: The Eyewitness Accounts of Major Rathbone and Clara Harris

Along with the president and Mrs. Lincoln, Major Henry Reed Rathbone and his fiancee, Clara Harris, were the only occupants of the presidential box at Ford's Theater on the night of April 14, 1865. Neither actually saw the fatal shot being fired. But as two of the persons closest to the scene of the assassination, their accounts of that evening are rich in detail and pathos.

Major Rathbone gave an affidavit the day following the murder. His testimony was as follows:

ON THE EVENING of the 14th of April last, at about twenty minutes past 8 o'clock, I, in company with Miss Harris, left my residence at the corner of Fifteenth and H Streets, and joined the President and Mrs. Lincoln, and went with them, in their carriage, to Ford's Theater, on Tenth Street. On reaching the theater, when the presence of the president became known, the actors stopped playing, the band struck up "Hail to the Chief," and the audience rose and received him with a vociferous cheering.

The party proceeded along in the rear of the dress-circle and entered the box that had been set apart for their reception. On entering the box, there was a large armchair that was placed nearest the audience, farthest from the stage, which the president took and occupied during the whole of the evening, with one exception, when he sat down again.

When the second scene of the third act was being performed, and while I was intently observing the proceedings upon the stage, with my back toward the door, I heard the discharge of a pistol behind me, and looking round, saw through the smoke a man between the door and the president.

The distance from the door to where the president sat was about four feet. At the same time I heard the man shout some word, which I thought was "Freedom!"

I instantly sprang toward him and seized him. He wrested himself from my grasp, and made a violent thrust at my breast with a large knife. I parried the blow by striking it up, and received a wound several inches deep in my left arm, between the elbow and the shoulder. The orifice of the wound was about an inch and a half in length, and extended upward

Major Henry Reed Rathbone.

toward the shoulder several inches. The man rushed to the front of the box and I endeavored to seize him again, but only caught his clothes as he was leaping over the railing of the box. The clothes, as I believe, were torn in the attempt to hold him. As he went over upon the stage, I cried out, "Stop that man." I then turned to the president, his position was not changed; his head was slightly bent forward, and his eyes were closed. I saw that he was unconscious, and, supposing him mortally wounded, rushed to the door for the purpose of calling medical aid.

On reaching the outer door of the passageway, I found it barred by a heavy piece of plank, one end of which was secured in the wall, and the other resting against the door. It had been so securely fastened that it required considerable force to remove it. This wedge or bar was about four feet from the floor. Persons upon the outside were beating against the door for the purpose of entering. I removed the bar, and the door was opened. Several persons, who represented themselves as surgeons, were allowed to enter. I saw there Colonel Crawford, and requested him to prevent other persons from entering the box.

I then returned to the box, and found the surgeons examining the president's person. They had not yet discovered the wound. As soon as it was discovered, it was determined to remove him from the theater. He was carried out, and I then proceeded to assist Mrs. Lincoln, who was intensely excited, to the stairs. I requested Major Potter to aid me in assisting Mrs. Lincoln across street to the house where the President was being conveyed. The wound which I had received had been bleeding very profusely, and on reaching the house, feeling very faint from the loss of blood, I seated myself in the hall, and soon after fainted away, and was laid upon the floor. Upon the return of consciousness I was taken to my residence.

Clara Harris.

In review of the transactions, it is my confident belief that the time which elapsed between the discharge of the pistol and the time when the assassin leaped from the box did not exceed thirty seconds. Neither Mrs. Lincoln nor Miss Harris had left their seats.

Harris, who also was deposed, later expanded on the horror of that evening in a letter written April 29, 1865:

YOU MAY WELL SAY that we have been passing through scenes sad indeed. That terrible Friday night is to me yet almost like some dreadful vision. I have been very intimate with Mrs. Lincoln and the family ever since our mutual residence in Washington, which began at the same time, and we have been constantly in the habit of driving and going to the opera and theater together. It was the only amusement, with the exception of receiving at their own house, in which the President and Mrs. Lincoln were permitted, according to custom, to indulge, and to escape from the crowds who constantly thronged to see them, more than from any decided taste for such things. They were in the habit of going very often to hear Forest, Booth, Hackett, and such actors, when playing in Washington.

The night before the murder was that of the general illumination here, and they drove all through the streets to see it; a less calculating villain might have taken that opportunity for his crime, or the night before, when the White House alone was brilliantly illuminated, and the figure of the president stood out in full relief to the immense crowd below, who stood in the darkness to listen to his speech. He spoke from the center window of the Executive Mansion. I had been invited to pass the evening there, and stood at the window in an adjoining room with Mrs. Lincoln, watching the crowd below as they listened and cheered. Of course Booth was there, watching his chance. I wonder he did not choose that occasion but probably he knew a better opportunity would be offered.

After the speech was over, we went into Mr. Lincoln's room; he was lying on the sofa, quite exhausted, but he talked of the events of the past fortnight, of his visit to Richmond, of the enthusiasm everywhere felt through the country; and Mrs. Lincoln declared the last few days to have been the happiest of her life. Their prospects indeed seemed fair—peace dawning upon our land, and four years of a happy and honored rule before one of the gentlest, best, and loveliest men I ever knew. I never saw him out of temper—the kindest husband, the tenderest father, the truest friend, as well as the wisest statesman. "Our beloved president"—when I think that I shall never again stand in his genial presence, that I lost his friendship so tried and true, I feel like putting on the robe of mourning which the country wears. . . .

We four composed the party that evening. They drove to our door in the gayest spirits; chatting on our way—and the president was received with the greatest enthusiasm.

They say we were watched by the assassins; ay, as we alighted from the carriage. Oh, how could any one be so cruel as to strike that kind, dear, honest face! And when I think of that fiend barring himself in alone with us, my blood runs cold. My dress is saturated with blood; my hands and face were covered. You may imagine what a scene! And so, all through that dreadful night, when we stood by that dying bed. Poor Mrs. Lincoln was and is almost crazy.

Henry narrowly escaped with his life. The knife struck at his heart with all the force of a practiced and powerful arm; he fortunately parried the blow, and received a wound in his arm, extending along the bone, from the elbow nearly to the shoulder. He concealed it for some time, but was finally carried home in swoon; the loss of blood has been so great from an artery and veins severed. He is now getting quite well, but cannot as yet use his arm.

SURRAT.   BOOTH.   HAROLD.

War Department, Washington, April 20, 1865,

$100,000 REWARD!

THE MURDERER

Of our late beloved President, Abraham Lincoln,

IS STILL AT LARGE.

$50,000 REWARD

Will be paid by this Department for his apprehension, in addition to any reward offered by Municipal Authorities or State Executives.

$25,000 REWARD

Will be paid for the apprehension of JOHN H. SURRATT, one of Booth's Accomplices.

$25,000 REWARD

Will be paid for the apprehension of David C. Harold, another of Booth's accomplices.

LIBERAL REWARDS will be paid for any information that shall conduce to the arrest of either of the above-named criminals, or their accomplices.

All persons harboring or secreting the said persons, or either of them, or aiding or assisting their concealment or escape, will be treated as accomplices in the murder of the President and the attempted assassination of the Secretary of State, and shall be subject to trial before a Military Commission and the punishment of DEATH.

Let the stain of innocent blood be removed from the land by the arrest and punishment of the murderers.

All good citizens are exhorted to aid public justice on this occasion. Every man should consider his own conscience charged with this solemn duty, and rest neither night nor day until it be accomplished.

EDWIN M. STANTON, Secretary of War.

DESCRIPTIONS.—BOOTH is Five Feet 7 or 8 inches high, slender build, high forehead, black hair, black eyes, and wears a heavy black moustache.

JOHN H. SURRAT is about 5 feet, 9 inches. Hair rather thin and dark; eyes rather light; no beard. Would weigh 145 or 150 pounds. Complexion rather pale and clear, with color in his cheeks. Wore light clothes of fine quality. Shoulders square; cheek bones rather prominent; chin narrow; ears projecting at the top; forehead rather low and square, but broad. Parts his hair on the right side; neck rather long. His lips are firmly set. A slim man.

DAVID C. HAROLD is five feet six inches high, hair dark, eyes dark, eyebrows rather heavy, full face, nose short, hand short and fleshy, feet small, instep high, round bodied, naturally quick and active, slightly closes his eyes when looking at a person.

NOTICE.—In addition to the above, State and other authorities have offered rewards amounting to almost one hundred thousand dollars, making an aggregate of about TWO HUNDRED THOUSAND DOLLARS

4

Manhunt

AT ABOUT THREE O'CLOCK ON THE AFTERNOON of April 24, 1865, ten days after the assassination, several men rode up to the yard gate of a farm near Port Royal, Virginia. The rider dressed in the uniform of a Confederate officer, eighteen-year-old Willie Jett, introduced himself and his companions to the owner of the property, Richard Henry Garrett.

"This is my friend, Mr. James W. Boyd, a Confederate soldier, who was wounded at the battle of Petersburg," Jett said of one weary, pasty-faced rider. "He is trying to get to his home in Maryland. Can you take care of him for a day or two until his wound will permit him to travel?"

Garrett, a religious man well known for his hospitality, had no objections. As the rest of the group rode off, the badly limping Boyd was given drink, a pillow, and a seat upon the verandah. Then he was left alone to sleep for several hours in his chair.

That evening Boyd joined the family for supper. The two oldest of Garrett's nine children, Jack and Willie, were veterans recently returned from the Appomattox campaign. Boyd, refreshed by his nap, impressed everyone at the table with his refined manner. Afterward, he tried to trade his dark suit of clothes for one of the older boys' worn Confederate uniforms. He explained that he wanted to join General Joseph Johnston's army, still fighting in North Carolina. "Now, as I am still to be a soldier and your battles are over," he said, "I will need a uniform, while you will need a suit."

The offer was politely refused. Soon afterward everybody turned in for the night, including the youngest Garrett, eleven-year-old Richard.

"The next morning when I arose," he recalled many years later, "I noticed for the first time hanging upon the post of the bed in which Mr. Boyd slept a belt, which held two large revolvers and a pearl-handled dirk or dagger, while lying on the mantel was a leather case containing a pair of opera glasses. The stranger was still sleeping, and as I dressed myself his face was turned toward me. I remember vividly the impression

Booth makes his escape down the alley in back of Ford's Theater as a member of the audience, Major J.B. Stewart, vainly gives chase.

made upon me at that time. I had never seen such a face before. Jet black curls clustered about a brow as white as marble, and a heavy dark mustache shaded a mouth as beautiful as a babe's. One hand was thrown above the head of the sleeper, and it was as white and soft as a child's. I was but a boy, but the thought came to me then that he was different from all the soldiers I had seen, for they were rough and tanned from exposure."

His suspicions grew the next day when he watched Boyd take down a map off the wall, then trace a route through Virginia, South Carolina, and Georgia. Where was he going, Richard wanted to know.

"To Mexico," Boyd answered.

"Why," responded the astonished boy, "I thought last night you were going to join Johnston's army in North Carolina."

Boyd said nothing. Neither did the boy, who watched as the mysterious visitor "traced a line from Charleston around through the Gulf of Mexico to Galveston, and from there he seemed to be uncertain as to his route into Mexico."

★

It had been a torturous ninety-five miles from Ford's Theater to Garrett's farm for John Wilkes Booth, alias James Boyd.

To begin with, his exit from the scene of the crime had been less graceful and more painful than planned. In jumping from the presidential box, he had snagged a spur in the Treasury Guard's colors, causing him to land awkwardly on the stage some ten feet below. Booth would later claim in a diary entry that this was when he snapped the small bone (fibula) of his lower left leg, just above the ankle. Whether this was the truth or a dramatic fabrication to make himself appear more heroic to future generations is still debated; a good deal of evidence points to Booth actually breaking his leg a few hours later, the result of his horse tumbling in the darkness and ingloriously falling over on him.

Broken leg or not, Booth quickly made it across the stage and through a door that led into the back alley of the theater. There "Peanuts John" Burroughs was obediently watching the assassin's horse for Edman Spangler, who was assisting with a scene change. Booth clambered aboard the skittish bay mare, struck the simple-minded errand boy with the butt of his knife, and whipped his mount into a gallop down the alley. He quickly outdistanced two pursuers: a theater carpenter named Jacob Rittersbaugh and Major Joseph B. Stewart, who had rushed out from the audience. His immediate destination was the Navy Yard Bridge, twenty minutes away. A few miles beyond that was the southern Maryland countryside.

Although the assaults on the president and the secretary of state had left Washington City in an uproar, news of the attacks did not keep pace with the galloping hooves of Booth's speedy little mare. At the Navy Yard Bridge he gave his real name to the sentry, who closely questioned him for several minutes before finally allowing him to cross the Anacostia River, the eastern branch of the Potomac. A short while later a second rider was permitted to thunder across the planks. It was David Herold, who was supposed to have guided Lewis Powell out of Washington, but who was now racing to find Booth in the darkness.

Secretary of War Edwin Stanton.

Herold caught up with Booth about eight miles south of the city. Their first stop was Mary Surratt's tavern in Surrattsville, where they picked up the two Spencer carbines, ammunition, and field glasses that had earlier been squirreled away. Before leaving, Booth told innkeeper John M. Lloyd, "I am pretty certain that we have assassinated the president and Secretary Seward."

After several hours of hard riding in the rain, Booth and Herold arrived at the farm of Dr. Samuel Mudd in Charles County, Maryland. It was about four o'clock Saturday morning, and the riders were tired and wet. Mudd, of course, was no stranger, having entertained Booth the previous year while the actor was mapping out an escape route for his abduction scheme. Mudd had also been responsible for introducing Booth to John Surratt.

Although Mudd was a Southern sympathizer and occasionally delivered mail for the Confederate underground, he neither trusted nor cared for Booth. Nonetheless, he agreed to do what he could for him, slitting Booth's high-top riding boot in order to set his fractured leg, then fitting him with a splint, a shoe, and a pair of crutches. Afterward the patient slept most of the day in an upstairs bedroom, his face to the wall, having said nothing of the assassination.

The Detroit Free Press.

VOLUME XXVIII.   DETROIT, MICHIGAN, SATURDAY MORNING, APRIL 15, 1865.   NUMBER 269.

THE LATEST

BY TELEGRAPH.

THE PRESIDENT ASSASSINATED.

He Is Shot at the Theatre

Escape of the Assassin.

HE SHOT FROM THE GALLERY, LEAPED TO THE STAGE WITH A GLEAMING KNIFE IN HIS HAND AND ESCAPED THROUGH THE BACK ENTRANCE.

HE THEN MOUNTED A HORSE AND FLED.

Before Leaving He Exclaimed "Sic Semper Tyrannus."

The President was Removed to a Private Residence and Died in a Short Time.

SECRETARY SEWARD ALSO ASSASSINATED.

HIS THROAT CUT, BUT IT IS HOPED HE WILL RECOVER.

TERRIBLE EXCITEMENT IN WASHINGTON.

THE RETREAT OF JOHNSTON.

The Detroit Free Press was typical of how newspapers treated news of the assassination, devoting most of its front page to the latest dispatches and trimming its columns in heavy black borders.

Meanwhile, Secretary of War Edwin Stanton had assumed control of the investigation and the reins of government. As the president lay dying in an upstairs bedroom of the Petersen House, Stanton was in the parlor questioning witnesses, reviewing options, and issuing orders. He was aided by provost marshals, detectives, and Union officers, all eager to join in the hunt. By early Saturday morning, cavalry troops were fanning out in all directions establishing roadblocks, searching houses, and rounding up hundreds of suspects.

As news of the assassination spread by telegraph to all parts of the country, millions of people expressed shock and outrage. Those who approved of the murder quickly learned to keep quiet about their feelings. Angry citizens beat—and occasionally killed—those insensitive enough to gloat or make light of their loss. Albert Daggett, who had been at Ford's Theater on Friday night, described the fate of one Lincoln-hater who had made

Dr. Mudd and his farmhouse as it appeared in 1901.

the mistake of saying that he was glad the president was shot. The "words had hardly left his mouth," Daggett wrote his wife, "before the bullet from the pistol of a Union soldier went crashing through his brain and his soul was summoned to the aweful presence of his maker with those horrible words upon his lips."

Booth family members had to deal with suspicion and derision. Junius, Jr., barely escaped a mob in Cincinnati, where he

was performing. Asia Booth Clarke was in bed inside her Philadelphia mansion, pregnant with twins, when she let out a shriek. The president had been shot, she learned from Saturday morning's newspaper, and her brother had been identified as the prime suspect. She suddenly remembered the package of materials John Wilkes had left a few months earlier in the safe. Among the items was his "To whom it may concern" letter, which Asia's husband, John Sleeper Clarke, gave to the press. Publication of this rambling political manifesto five days after the murder not only removed doubt as to the identity of the assassin, it increased suspicion directed toward the family. Soon Junius Booth, Jr., and John Sleeper Clarke were arrested and thrown into Old Capitol Prison, where they would be held without charges for the next several weeks. Detectives kept close tabs on other family members. Meanwhile, dozens of men matching John Wilkes Booth's description were picked up in cities around the country.

Booth spent most of the day following the assassination in Dr. Mudd's upstairs bedroom, resting his hobbled leg. He occupied the bed on the right; much of the time his face was to the wall.

On Saturday afternoon, April 15, while the real Booth slept and thousands of Union troops crawled over the countryside, Dr. Mudd headed for the village of Bryantown, four miles away, to run some errands. Herold, hoping to find a buggy to transport Booth, accompanied him. However, he became unnerved by the sight of a detachment of cavalrymen and headed back to Mudd's farm. A couple of hours later Mudd returned, furious over the news he had heard in Bryantown. Being party to an abduction was one thing; aiding assassins was quite another. Booth had put the doctor and his entire family at risk. Mudd demanded that the two fugitives leave his property, which they quickly did.

Two days later, upon the advice of a cousin in whom he had confided, Mudd went to authorities in Bryantown and told them a vague story about his contact with "a stranger" with a broken limb. Mudd initially denied that the man was Booth—a lie that would wind up costing him dearly. On April 21, one week after the assassination, detectives discovered Booth's slit riding boot inside Mudd's house. This damning piece of evidence got Mudd arrested as an accomplice. More important, it allowed the government to concentrate its efforts on "lame man" sightings, which narrowed the field of suspects considerably.

By then the fugitives were hiding out in the dismal wilderness of Zekiah Swamp, looking for their chance to cross the Potomac River into Virginia. This normally would have been a simple matter. Before the assassination Confederate agents had crisscrossed the river with almost ridiculous ease, thanks to the cooperation of the local populace, which was notoriously pro-Southern. But now an ever-growing number of Union troops was in the area, manhandling residents and treating them as "traitors" as they combed the countryside and riverbanks for the fugitives.

Thomas A. Jones, the chief Confederate agent in the region, sheltered Booth and Herold for several days before arranging for their trip across the Potomac. In addition to providing food, Jones supplied Booth with daily newspapers, which he read with great interest—and deep anguish. Far from understanding and approving of the assassination, as Booth thought would be the case, newspapers condemned it as a despicable, cowardly act and called for the swift apprehension—and slow death—of the persons responsible.

Those closest to Booth vacillated between horror and disbelief over his identification as the president's murderer. The women in his life seemed particularly affected. His mother and sister, Asia, reeled from the shock inside the Philadelphia mansion. Actress Ella Starr, who kept a photograph of him under her pillow, tried to commit suicide the day after the assassination. His fiancee, Lucy Hale, was "plunged in profoundest grief," reported the *New York Tribune*, "but with womanly fidelity, is slow to believe him guilty of this appalling crime, and asks, with touching pathos, for evidence of his innocence."

The Garrett farmhouse, on whose porch Booth died. The assassin's last words were, "Useless . . . useless."

At this time Booth—hollow-eyed, aching, and shivering inside Zekiah Swamp—actually was preparing evidence of his guilt, in the form of a human document that sought to rationalize his deed. The following passages appeared in a small 1864 pocket diary that he had been carrying around to record addresses, financial notes, and other memoranda. With no other paper available, Booth ripped out the first several pages and began scrawling his thoughts. His dating of the first entry, which was written several days after the event, referred to Caesar's assassination on the Ides of March.

APRIL 14 FRIDAY THE IDES

Until today nothing was ever thought of sacrificing to our country's wrongs. For six months we had worked to capture. But our cause, being almost lost, something decisive & great must be done. But its failure was owing to others, who did not strike for their country with a heart. I struck boldly and not as the papers say. I walked with a fine step through a thousand of his friends, was stopped, but pushed on. A colonel was at his side. I shouted Sic semper before I fired. In jumping broke my leg. I passed all his pickets, rode sixty miles that night, with the bone of my leg tearing the flesh at every jump. I can never repent it, though we hated to kill. Our country owed all her

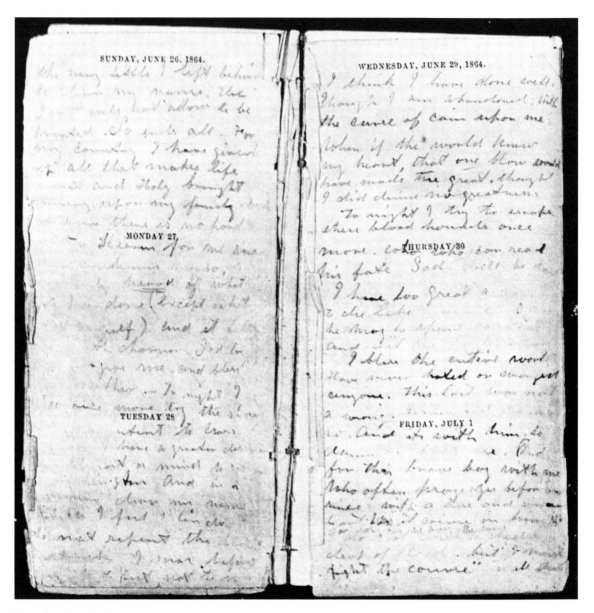

Pages from Booth's diary.

trouble to him, and God simply made me the instrument of his punishment. The country is not—April 1865 what it was. This forced union is not what I have loved. I care not what becomes of me. I have no desire to outlive my country. . . .

After being hunted like a dog through swamps, woods, and last night being chased by gun boats till I was forced to return wet, cold, and starving, with every man's hand against me, I am here in despair. And why? For doing what Brutus was honored for. What made Tell a Hero. And yet I for striking down a greater tyrant than—they ever knew am looked upon as a common cutthroat. My action was purer than either of theirs. One hoped to be great himself. The other had not only his country's but his own wrongs to avenge. I hoped for no gain. I knew no private wrong. I struck for my country and that alone. A country groaned beneath this tyranny and prayed for this end, and yet now behold the cold hand they extend to me. God cannot pardon me if I have done wrong. Yet I cannot see any wrong except in serving a degenerate people. The little—the very little I left behind to clear my name, the Govmt will not allow to be printed. So ends all. For my country I have given up all that makes life sweet and Holy, brought misery upon my family and am sure there is no pardon—in the Heaven for me since man condemns me so. I have only heard of what has been done (except what I did myself) and it fills me with horror. God try and forgive me, and bless my mother. Tonight I will once more try the river with the intent to cross; though I have a greater desire and almost a mind to return to Washington and in a measure clear my name, which I feel I can do. I do not repent the blow I struck. I may before my God but not to man. I think I have done well, though I am abandoned, with the curse of Cain upon me, when if the world knew my heart, that one blow would have made me great, though I did desire no greatness. Tonight I try to escape these blood hounds once more. Who, who can read his fate God's will be done. I have too great a soul to die like a criminal. O may he, may he spare me that and let me die bravely. I bless the entire world. Have never hated or wronged anyone. This last was not a wrong, unless God deems it—so. And it's with him to damn or bless me. And for this brave boy with me who often prays (yes, before and since) with a true and sincere heart. Was it crime in him, if so, why can he pray the same? I do not wish to shed a drop of blood, but "I must fight the course." 'Tis all that's left me.

Booth, who was resigned to dying rather than surrendering to authorities, clearly was writing for posterity's sake. In an attempt to make himself appear as heroic as possible, he inflated his account of the murder and his escape. He stated that he shoved his way past a colonel to get at Lincoln, broke his leg upon jumping from the presidential box, and rode sixty miles that first night—all of which was untrue. His second entry, written after he and Herold had finally crossed into Virginia in a skiff provided by Jones, also took a good deal of liberty with the facts.

To their surprise, Booth and Herold received a lukewarm reception from the Virginians they came in contact with. Most, though loyal to the Confederate cause, were afraid of the consequences of housing or otherwise aiding the fugitives. On the evening of April 23 they forced their way into the one-room cabin of a free-born black named William Lucas, kicking him and his sick wife out at knifepoint. The following morning they had Lucas's son drive them to Port Conway on the Rappahannock River, about ten miles away. From there the pair arranged with a fisherman, William Rollins, to be ferried over to Port Royal on the opposite shore.

While they were awaiting passage, three young Confederate soldiers—Willie Jett, Absalom Ruggles Bainbridge, and Mortimer Bainbridge Ruggles—rode up to the ferry landing. After unsuccessfully trying to convince the riders that he and Booth were two soldiers trying to join troops still fighting in the South, Herold admitted, "We are the assassinators of the president." Jett was so impressed he asked for an autograph.

Once in Port Royal, Jett tried to leave the badly injured Booth at the home of a local planter, but the owner's sister quickly revoked her offer of Southern hospitality upon sight of the filthy, unshaven guest. She suggested visiting the nearby farm of Richard Henry Garrett, whose home was open to everyone. So it was that John Wilkes Booth wound up spending the last two days of his life as the guest of a family which did not discover his true identity until the very end.

★

As James W. Boyd (an alias Booth chose to match the J.W.B. initials tattooed on his hand), the injured and exhausted guest

⊰ Lincoln: A Color Gallery of His Life and Death ⊱

Louis Bonhajo emphasized various aspects of the Lincoln legend in a series of a dozen paintings, including the pioneer, the storyteller, and the country lawyer.

A Currier & Ives print from the 1860 presidential election. The Republican ticket included Lincoln and Senator Hannibal Hamlin

This life-size portrait of Lincoln the rail-splitter was created by an unknown artist in 1860.

In his 1862 cartoon, Lincoln Crushing the Dragon of Rebellion, *David Gilmour Blythe* borrowed from a familiar theme to show the new president smashing secession with a rail-splitter's maul.

"The Great Emancipator" often was depicted in classically heroic terms, as in S.N. Carvalho's portrait and A.A. Lamb's Emancipation Proclamation.

G.P.A. Healy's painting, The Peacemakers, *shows an 1865 meeting of the commander in chief and his senior officers: Generals William T. Sherman and Ulysses S. Grant and Admiral David D. Porter.*

Gustav Bartsch's stylized depiction of Lincoln's visit to City Point, Virginia, in the closing weeks of the war was stirring but woefully inaccurate. The president arrived by ship, not on horseback, and the city was a bustling Union depot, not a recently liberated Confederate stronghold.

Carte-de-visite *photographs, introduced in 1859 and named after the French visiting card, were immensely popular during the 1860s. Admirers of the president collected likenesses of him, his family, and even his horse, in albums.*

This stereograph of a tired and sorrowful Lincoln was taken in early 1865, just weeks before his assassination.

The assassin, his infamous deed, and his ignominious end inside a burning barn in Virginia.

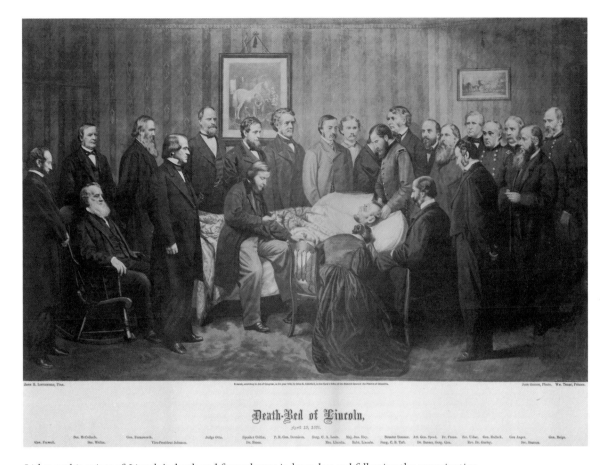

Death-Bed of Lincoln,

Lithographic prints of Lincoln's death and funeral were in huge demand following the assassination.

THE CATAFALQUE, OR HEARSE,

AS SEEN IN THE FUNERAL PROCESSION OF PRESIDENT LINCOLN.

Published by H. H. Lloyd & Co., 21 John St., New York.

The country's grief was captured in countless versions of folk art. They ranged from mass-produced carte-de-visite *views, like "Columbia's Grief," to such impromptu tableaux as the one an anonymous mourner rendered in ink and watercolor on a page torn from a ledger.*

Lincoln, the first president to be assassinated, later was joined in martyrdom by James Garfield and William McKinley, fellow Republicans who were murdered in office in 1881 and 1901, respectively.

received hospitable treatment from the Garretts. On his second day there, April 25, news of the assassination finally reached the isolated farm, though the name of the murderer was unknown and the senior Garrett dismissed the report as just a rumor. Booth coyly asked about the size of the reward being offered. Told that it was $100,000, he replied, "That is not as much as I expected them to offer."

"That man had better not come this way," joked one of Garrett's soldier-sons, "for I would like to make $100,000 just now."

"Would you betray him for that?" asked Booth.

"He had better not tempt me," was the response, "for I haven't a dollar in the world."

About four o'clock that Tuesday afternoon, Herold and his three Confederate companions rode up to the gate, after having spent the previous day and night socializing in the village of Bowling Green, several miles down the road. After Jett, Ruggles, and Bainbridge left, Booth introduced his co-conspirator to the Garretts as his cousin, "Mr. Harris." Their suspicions were aroused, however, when two of the men soon returned, shouting, "The Yankees are crossing the river at Port Royal," before galloping off again.

The Yankees were a detachment of the 16th New York Cavalry, commanded by Lieutenant Edward P. Doherty. In addition to the twenty-six cavalrymen, the group included a pair of hard-nosed detectives, Everton Conger and Luther Baker, both former Union officers. They had learned from William Rollins of the fugitives' crossing of the Rappahannock the previous day. Now the unit was heading towards Bowling Green, passing right past the Garrett farm as Booth and Herold hid in the woods, weapons at the ready.

Their guests' odd reaction was too much for the Garretts, who confronted them after they came out of hiding. They refused Booth's offer to buy their horses but, anxious to see their guests leave, arranged for them to borrow a neighbor's wagon the following morning. Meanwhile, the visitors were told that they were no longer welcome in their home. After much pleading, Booth and Herold finally were allowed to spend the night inside the tobacco barn. "I am afraid these men will get us into trouble," Richard Garrett told sons Jack and Willie. "You had better watch them tonight." Unbeknownst to

Booth and Herold, the Garrett boys locked the barn behind them, then secreted themselves in a nearby corn crib in order to keep an eye on them.

Around midnight, Doherty's men quietly surrounded the Star Hotel in Bowling Green, where Herold and his new friends had spent the previous day. Everton Conger burst into the front parlor, where Willie Jett was sleeping, and, holding him at the point of a .44-caliber service revolver, he quickly found out where Booth and Herold were spending the night. By two o'clock Wednesday morning the search party had dismounted and been deployed around the Garrett farm.

When Richard Garrett came to the door in his nightshirt to find out what all the commotion was about, Luther Baker shoved his pistol in the old man's face and demanded, "Where are they?" Stunned and frightened, Garrett tried to tell the detective about a Mr. Boyd and the woods, but Baker cut him short. "I don't want any long story out of you," he said. "I just want to know where those men have gone."

A trooper led an equally bewildered Jack Garrett, discovered behind the house, to Lieutenant Doherty. Doherty grabbed a fistful of Garrett's shirt and demanded to know the whereabouts of the fugitives. Already the Garretts' stammering had the party threatening to hang them from the nearest locust tree. The men they were looking for were in the tobacco shed, Jack Garrett said.

The barn, about fifty yards from the house, was immediately surrounded. "You men had better come out here," Baker shouted, pounding on the double door with the butt of his revolver.

"Who are you?" Booth yelled.

"Never mind who we are," Baker replied. "We know who you are. You had better come out and deliver yourselves up." Then he shoved Jack Garrett through the door and into the barn. The terrified young man told Booth to give up, that resistance was useless. "You have betrayed me!" Booth responded. "Damn you!" Garrett was certain that Booth would shoot him, but Baker opened the door and let him scramble out before slamming it shut again.

At this point Baker, Conger, and Doherty discussed strategy. Doherty was all for waiting until daylight until forcing the men out, but the detectives were impatient. If Booth and Herold didn't come out in ten minutes, Baker announced, they would set the barn on fire.

This was too much for Herold, who wanted to surrender. "You damn coward!" responded his disgusted companion. "Will you leave me now?"

But Herold continued to plead and Booth finally relented. "Surrender if you want," the assassin said, "but I will fight and die like a man."

Booth then called out, "There is a man in here who wants to surrender very much." Herold stuck his arms through the door, whereupon troopers seized him and then tied him to a nearby tree. Booth insisted that Herold was an innocent and unwilling participant. Going along with this fiction, Herold told his captors, "I know nothing of this man," a story that Jack Garrett quickly repudiated.

More time passed. Booth, who had three pistols and a carbine at his disposal, asked for a sporting chance to shoot it out, a request Baker denied. Instead Conger twisted some hay into a rope, lit it, and threw it through a slat in the back of the barn.

If Booth hoped to go out in a blaze of glory, he quickly found himself trapped inside a literal version of his wish. The barn, filled with wooden furniture that the Garretts were storing for their neighbors, exploded into flames.

"It was a fearful picture," recalled young Richard Garrett. "Framed in great waves of fire stood the crippled man leaning upon his crutches and holding his carbine in his hand. His hat had fallen off and his hair was brushed back from his white forehead. He was as beautiful as the statue of a Greek god and as calm in that awful hour."

It was at this moment that Sergeant Thomas "Boston" Corbett, as odd a figure as ever crossed the pages of American history, stepped into the story. Seven years earlier the devout Methodist, a hatter by trade, had recited from the Gospel of Matthew to several prostitutes before going home and cutting off his testicles with a pair of scissors. According to Corbett's file in the War Department, "He then went to a prayer meeting, walked about some, and ate a hearty dinner." Only then did he have himself sutured by a doctor.

Corbett was "later accepted into the United States Cavalry," continued his file, "where he distinguished himself by the ferocity of his fighting, his earlier self-mutilation apparently being no handicap to the performance of his soldierly duties." The long-haired, slightly built cavalryman's fanaticism for doing the Lord's work carried over to combat. In an action against Mosby's Rangers near Culpepper, Virginia, he smote seven of the enemy before being captured, reportedly taking time to rejoice as each rebel fell, "Amen! Glory to God!"

In the early morning hours of April 26, 1865, Corbett once again played the role of avenging angel. As Booth made a move towards the barn door, a carbine in one hand and a revolver in the other, a shot rang out. The assassin pitched face-first to the ground, then rolled partly over.

Booth was dragged like a sack of seed away from the burning barn and placed on the porch of the Garrett farmhouse.

He was paralyzed. The bullet had passed through the right side of his neck, shattering several vertebrae and cutting his spinal cord. The Garrett women brought out a mattress and pillows and tried to make him as comfortable as possible, and a rag was soaked with water and placed in his mouth, but nothing could change the fact that he had suffered a mortal wound.

In the confusion it was initially thought that Booth had shot himself. Later it was determined that Corbett, standing a few yards away and alarmed by Booth's sudden movement, had shot his revolver through one of the shed's wide slats. As Booth lay dying, Corbett was ferociously upbraided by his superiors, who had wanted to bring the assassin back alive.

"Why in hell did you shoot without orders?" one demanded to know. The emasculated avenger replied that "Providence" had directed him. "I aimed at his shoulder," Corbett later offered in his defense. "I did not want to kill him. . . . I think he stooped to pick up something just as I fired. That may probably account for his receiving the ball in the head."

For the next two and a half hours Booth drifted in and out of consciousness. He begged his captors to kill him. At one point he told Baker, "Tell my mother—tell my mother I did it for my country—that I die for my country."

A doctor was sent for from Port Royal, but he could do nothing. As the sun rose, announcing a new day, Booth asked to see his hands. His purple lips moved one last time. "Useless," he murmured. "Useless."

★

After his death Booth was positively identified in a field examination. In addition to his distinctive tattoo and personal effects (which included his diary), his likeness matched that on the photographs carried by his pursuers. Lieutenant Doherty, who in the past had often roomed at the same Washington City hotel as Booth, the National, knew the actor by sight. David Herold admitted that the man the Garretts had known as John Boyd was really John Wilkes Booth.

The Garretts were astounded. "This was positively the first intimation that any of us had as to who our guests were," Richard Garrett stressed in a popular lecture he gave years later. "Standing beside the dead body, my father heard for the first time that the man who for two days had been his guest was the man who had killed the president."

The assassin's identity was confirmed in an autopsy conducted aboard the ironclad *Montauk* on April 27, with Booth's dentist and doctor testifying to certain tell-tale physical characteristics. Afterward, on the orders of Secretary of War Stanton, the shriveled body was sewn inside a tarpaulin, placed into a guncase, and secretly buried beneath the floor of the ammunition room of the Old Penitentiary. There it would stay for four years, until being released to relatives for burial in the Booth family plot in Baltimore.

Lucy Hale was devastated by word of Booth's death. During the two-week manhunt friends of Senator Hale had attempted damage control, denying that there ever was an engagement between the senator's daughter and the fugitive assassin. Members of both families knew better. Edwin Booth wrote his sister, Asia: "I have had a heart-broken letter from the poor little girl to whom he had promised so much happiness." Lucy had no choice but to accept that her beloved John Wilkes—who at the time of his death was carrying on his person pictures of her and four other women, all actresses—was not the man she had thought he was. She subsequently married William E. Chandler, who, like her father, was a respected senator from New Hampshire.

April 26, 1865: John Wilkes Booth, mortally wounded, is dragged out of a burning barn at Garrett's Farm, near Port Royal, Virginia. To the right in this drawing from Leslie's Illustrated Newspaper *is David Herold, who, much to Booth's disgust, had earlier surrendered rather than fight the contingent of soldiers that surrounded them.*

Was the body in the barn really Booth? Fanciful stories of mistaken identity or the assassin's escape would swirl around for years and are still held fast to by a diehard few. One true believer was a fifteen-year-old actress, Kitty Brink, who had been at Ford's Theater the night of the murder. "The man they got in that barn was not Booth," she was still insisting in 1935, seventy years after the assassin's final exit. "Of course, I can't prove it definitely one way or another, but I, and a great number of others who knew him, have always been convinced that he got away and died under another name many years later."

But Sergeant Andrew Wendell and the rest of Doherty's command knew better. "On the boat going up to Washington with the body," recalled Wendell, "we troopers all filed past and had a good look. Some people—and big people—said that we had the wrong man and that Booth wasn't dead. He was dead enough when we looked at him."

★

The secretive and unceremonious manner in which Booth's body was handled and then disposed of was a far cry from the reverential treatment accorded the slain president. During the time in which the conspirators were zealously tracked down and rounded up, millions of Americans shared in an elaborate sendoff unprecedented in the nation's history. Those who didn't actively participate in the drawn-out, cross-country

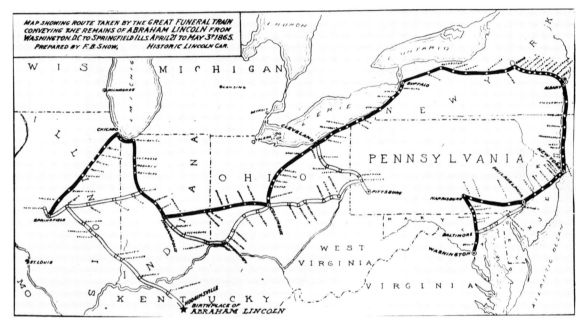

MAP SHOWING ROUTE TAKEN BY THE GREAT FUNERAL TRAIN CONVEYING THE REMAINS OF ABRAHAM LINCOLN FROM WASHINGTON.D.C. TO SPRINGFIELD ILLS APRIL 21 TO MAY 3rd 1865. PREPARED BY F.B. SNOW,   HISTORIC LINCOLN CAR.

The route of the Great Funeral Train that took Lincoln home. Between April 21 and May 3, it stopped for funeral services in ten cities before arriving in Springfield.

funeral services grieved in their own fashion—through prayers, by placing homemade tributes on the parlor table, or by buying black-edged cards to put in the family album. Countless citizens wore mourning ribbons with the president's likeness.

Lincoln's journey from his deathbed to his final resting place in Springfield proved as long and winding as any he had taken years earlier as a lawyer riding the circuit. Shortly after expiring, his body was removed from the Petersen House to the second-floor guest room at the White House, where two army pathologists—Assistant Surgeon J. Janvier Woodward and Assistant Surgeon Edward Curtis—performed the autopsy. They began by sawing off the top of the president's skull above the ears.

Then, recalled Dr. Curtis, "Dr. Woodward and I proceeded to open the head and remove the brain down to the track of

Tuesday, April 18, 1865: After a somber service inside the White House, the funeral procession marches up Pennsylvania Avenue to Capitol Hill, where Lincoln's body will lie in state before beginning a two-week, 1,700-mile journey back to Springfield.

the ball. The latter had entered a little to the left of the median line at the back of the head, had passed almost directly towards the center of the brain and lodged. Not finding it readily, we proceeded to remove the entire brain, when, as I was lifting the latter from the cavity of the skull, suddenly the bullet dropped out through my fingers and fell, breaking the solemn silence of the room with its clatter, into an empty basin that was standing beneath. There it lay upon the white china, a little black mass no bigger than the end of my finger—dull, motionless, and harmless, yet the cause of such mighty changes in the world's history as we may perhaps never realize."

After the autopsy was completed, Lincoln became the latest beneficiary of an advance made in mortuary science that was a direct result of the Civil War. Undertakers, faced with the task of transporting the bodies of dead soldiers long distances from the battlefields back to their hometowns for final burial, had made great strides in embalming as a method of controlling decay. Now, undertaker Dr. Charles D. Brown drained Lincoln's blood through his jugular vein, then pumped a chemical solution through a cut on the inside of the leg. "He lies in sleep," observed one reporter in describing the embalming, "but it is the sleep of marble. All that made this flesh vital, sentient and affectionate is gone forever."

He was shaved and, after spending Easter Sunday and Monday on the embalmer's cooling table, dressed in the black suit he had worn at his second inauguration. Placed inside an ornate walnut casket that cost $1,500, the president was once again ready to face his public.

On April 18, a line of mourners one mile long and six people abreast formed outside the White House. They silently awaited their turn to file past the open casket, which had been placed upon an imposing catafalque (called the "Temple of Death") inside the dimly lit East Room. The following day, a warm, radiant Wednesday fragrant with the perfume of blossoming lilacs and magnolias, an estimated sixty thousand people lined the streets of Washington to watch a procession of some forty

The only known photograph of Lincoln in his coffin was taken by Jeremiah Gurney on April 24 inside New York City Hall. Secretary of War Stanton, incensed that Gurney planned to sell copies to the public, ordered the plates seized and destroyed. However, a single print survived. It remained undiscovered until 1952.

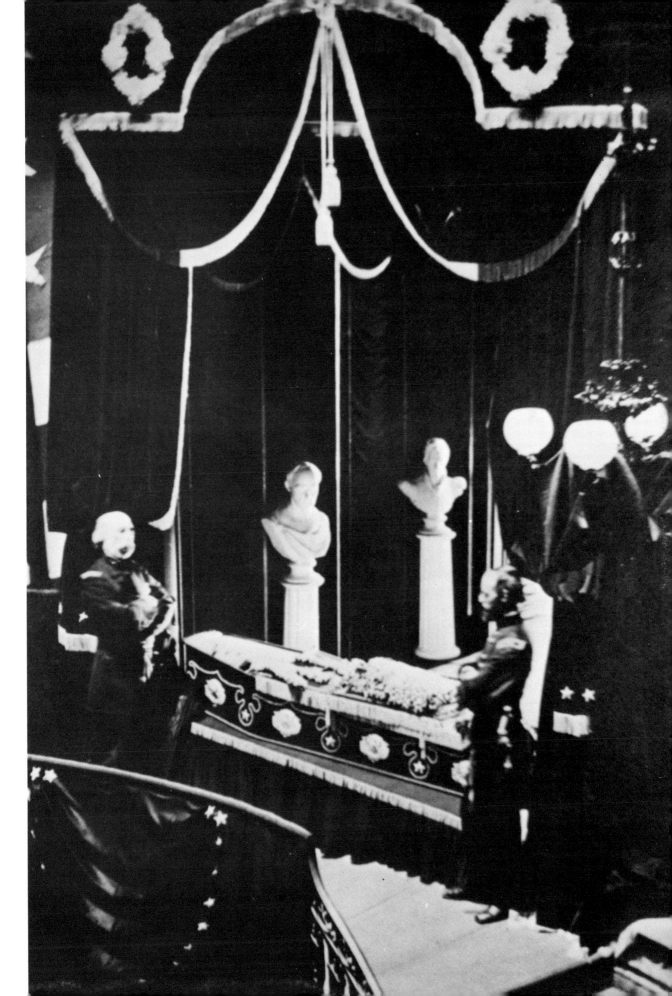

thousand march the one and a half miles from the White
House, where the official funeral service was conducted, to
Capitol Hill, where he was to lie in state in the rotunda until
Friday. Cannons boomed and bells tolled as the coffin, carried
on a funeral car drawn by six white horses, slowly rolled past a
community awash in black crepe. Among the marchers were
four thousand Negro citizens, wearing white gloves and silk
hats and solemnly walking hand in hand down Pennsylvania
Avenue. It was an incredibly moving day. But the Washington
funeral (which cost taxpayers $30,000) was only the beginning
of the organized mourning.

Earlier in the week, a delegation of Illinois residents had successfully lobbied Mary Lincoln to have her husband buried in
Springfield, instead of in Washington or Chicago, her first two
choices. It was decided that the train back to Illinois would follow, in reverse, the same route President-elect Lincoln had
taken when he had come to Washington four years earlier. The
only change would be the omission of Cincinnati, which was
judged to be too far south. What followed was an epic,
unprecedented two-week journey during which the Lincoln
funeral train traveled 1,700 miles and stopped for services in ten
cities before arriving at its final destination.

The first stop was Baltimore. On Friday morning, April 21, at
the same time that the city's most infamous son was desperately eluding his pursuers in the marshes on the
Maryland-Virginia border, the nine-car train pulled into the
rain-swept station. The first seven cars held three hundred relatives and dignitaries, and the last car contained their baggage.
In the second-from-last car were the coffins containing Lincoln
and his disinterred son, Willie, watched by a stone-faced honor
guard. The engine was draped in black, and a large black-
trimmed portrait of the president was attached to the
cowcatcher. It was preceded by a pilot engine, which throughout the cross-country journey traveled ahead to make sure
the track was clear. As would be the case at every stop along
the way, tens of thousands of the sorrowful and the curious
turned out.

The casket was carefully removed from the car by a contingent of Veterans Corps sergeants and placed into an ornate
hearse. An enormous procession of civic leaders, military

units, and ordinary citizens accompanied it to a tastefully prepared public place, where it was placed on an elaborate
catafalque and then opened for viewing. Twin ranks of mourners were ushered quickly past, though not too fast for some to
attempt to touch the president's body, kiss the coffin, or place

*In city after city, the scene was the
same: marchers, bands, tolling bells,
and miles of black crepe. Ornate
funeral cars, such as this one
designed and built by the Buffalo
firm of Cheeseman & Dodge, were
specially made to receive and transport the president's remains.*

something inside the casket. Then it was back to the depot and
the resumption of the long overland voyage home.

Over the next dozen days the routine, with occasional varia-
tions, was repeated at Harrisburg, Philadelphia, New York,
Albany, Buffalo, Cleveland, Columbus, Indianapolis, and
Chicago. There was even an impromptu funeral service conducted inside the president's railroad car during an
unscheduled stop at Michigan City, Indiana. The funeral commission in each city strove to stage the most expensive pageant,
construct the grandest catafalque, and deliver the most elo-
quent eulogy.

This drawn-out public exhibition of grief raised the hackles
of many Southerners, who saw it as a way of stoking animos-
ity towards their defeated nation. But for the million or so
people who braved rainstorms, pickpockets, unruly crowds,
long lines, interminable waits, and overzealous policemen for a
fleeting glimpse of the president's mortal remains, it repre-

sented a form of closure. Their number included several past
and future chief executives. The fifteenth president, James
Buchanan, a day shy of his seventy-fourth birthday, drove his
buggy from his estate in Lancaster, Pennsylvania, to the depot
to see the train bearing his successor slowly glide by on its way
to Philadelphia. In New York, six-year-old Theodore Roosevelt
leaned out a second-story window and watched the 120,000-
man marching spectacle pass his grandfather's house on
Broadway. In Buffalo, the lines of mourners included the thirteenth president, Millard Fillmore, who the previous year had
campaigned for General McClellan, and a young lawyer named
Grover Cleveland, whose decision to send a substitute to fight
during the war so he could support his widowed mother would
not prevent him from being elected to two terms in the White
House.

What occurred between scheduled stops was equally remarkable. Every depot along the way had some form of tribute, whether it was signs carrying mottoes such as HE STILL
LIVES or THE ILLUSTRIOUS MARTYR OF LIBERTY; a lighted
arch of evergreen boughs; or a patriotic tableau, such as a
young woman dressed as Lady Liberty mourning over a mock
coffin. Most of the population of each town and village turned
out to sing, salute, doff hats, and strew flowers along the track.
Farmers knelt in muddy fields as the train slowly chugged
through the countryside at a steady twenty miles per hour. At
night, people lit up the darkness with torches, bonfires, and
candles, showing Father Abraham the way home.

Two weeks of muffled drumbeats, soft singing, and ringing
church bells came to an end on May 4, when the caskets of the
president and his son were placed inside a vault at Oak Hill
Cemetery in Springfield. It was none too soon, for Lincoln's
shockingly black and shriveled face had needed regular pow-
dering from Dr. Brown. His lips, as originally positioned by the
undertaker, remained slightly upturned, giving him an expression of mild amusement over the commotion his passing had
caused.

The country had never seen anything like the Lincoln
funeral train before, and there hasn't been anything quite like
the "black pageant" since. It spawned a new American tradition: the giving of flowers at funerals. Previously, they had

been reserved for celebrating happy occasions. But in the spring of 1865, a huge number of Americans, casting about for a way to express their sorrow, settled on bouquets of sacrificial flowers. The sweet, melancholic perfume of lilies, lilacs, roses, and orange blossoms was everywhere that spring. It was entirely fitting that when poet Walt Whitman, who cared for wounded soldiers in Washington during the war, sat down to write of the nation's loss, he entitled his work "When Lilacs Last in the Dooryard Bloom'd."

The Lincoln funeral train also became a powerful piece of American folklore. For many years afterward, railroad hands along the route told stories of the Lincoln ghost train, an apparition that would appear on the anniversary of its original passage. The *Albany Evening Times* once described the legend:

Home at last. On May 4, 1865, the remains of the martyred president and his disinterred son, Willie, were laid to rest at Oak Ridge Cemetery in Springfield.

On either side of the tracks it is warm and still. Every watchman, when he feels the air, slips off the track and sits down to watch. Soon the pilot engine of Lincoln's funeral train passes with long, black streamers and with a band of black instruments playing dirges, grinning skeletons sitting all about. . . . If

In contrast to Lincoln's elaborate send-off, Booth was secretly and unceremoniously buried beneath the floor of the ammunition room of the Old Penitentiary. The assassin's body would stay there for four years before being released to his family.

it is moonlight, clouds come over the moon as the phantom train goes by. After the pilot engine passes, the funeral train itself with flags and streamers rushes past. The track seems covered with black carpet, and the coffin is seen in the center of the car, while all about it in the air and on the train behind are vast numbers of blue-coated men, some with coffins on their backs, others leaning upon them.

Clocks and watches react to the train gliding silently past, the story continued. When looked at again, they are always several minutes behind.

Sideshow: The Mythic Afterlife of John Wilkes Booth

⊰ BY MICHAEL W. KAUFFMAN ⊱

THE LINCOLN ASSASSINATION has spawned more than its share of folk-tales. One of the most persistent is the legend that John Wilkes Booth was not killed in 1865. History tells us that on April 26, 1865, Booth was trapped in a Virginia tobacco barn by members of the 16th New York Cavalry. The barn was set on fire, and Booth was shot as he tried to make a break for the door. Wounded in the neck, he died a few hours later on the front porch of Richard Garrett's house. His corpse was wrapped in an army blanket and taken back to the capital, where it was buried on the grounds of the Washington Arsenal. It remained there for four years, until the assassin's family moved it to Baltimore.

Only hours after Booth died, stories began to circulate that the wrong man had been killed at Garrett's farm. An inquest held over the body might have put such rumors to rest, but Colonel Lafayette C. Baker ruined any chance of that. Baker—chief of the national detective police and a self-styled master of disinformation—caused a stir among the media by leaving the scene of Booth's autopsy in a small rowboat, then pretending to dump a corpse into the Potomac River. What seemed unexplainable to some was merely a habit for Baker. He would later call this act a security measure.

Over the next few years phantom sightings would place Booth in South America, Ceylon, Europe, and Mexico. But these reports never panned out, nor were they ever taken seriously. The American public was quite satisfied that Abraham Lincoln's death had indeed been avenged in 1865. The Booth family's own identification of the remains in 1869 seemed to erase any lingering doubt on the part of the public. But there were exceptions.

Shortly after the war's end, a Mississippi family harbored a man they thought was Booth on his way to Mexico. In 1871, a Tennessee woman nursed another "Booth" through his final illness, and yet another "Booth" took his wedding vows a few months after that. Whether he appeared as a farmer in Mississippi or a photographer in California, John Wilkes Booth was sighted often throughout the South and West. He could always be spotted easily enough: he was the dark-haired stranger in town who recited Shakespeare, limped about, and carried himself with an air of mystery.

Taking a closer look, we discover that most of these men had never really claimed to be Booth. That was just the rumor, helped along by the fact that most folks in the West were new to the area. But once in a while, some pathetic soul would let his loneliness get the better of him, and he would blurt out his "true" identity to a trusted friend. The ruse often worked, and the new "Booth" became the talk of the town.

Enter David E. George. On the morning of January 13, 1903, this middle-aged alcoholic locked himself into a cramped hotel room in Enid, Oklahoma, and ended his life with poison. The afternoon edition of the *Enid Wave* told of George's despondency and gave the details of his suicide. His money was gone, and he seemed to have no prospects. So now he was dead, but that turned out to be the beginning, not the end, of his story.

Reading a press account of George's death, a local woman remarked to her husband that she had once known a man by the name of George in El Reno. He was a strange man, she recalled, once telling her that he was really John Wilkes Booth. Reverend Enoch Harper was intrigued. He told his wife's story to the undertaker, who happened to be a former editor for the *New York Sun*. In no time at all, a media circus was underway.

Thirty-eight years had passed since Lincoln's assassination, and during this period plenty of Booth survival legends had come and gone. Many of these originated in the Old West, whose transient culture made the region a perfect place for outlaws and outcasts to disappear. Anonymity didn't sit well with some of these characters, who often spread rumors to inflate their notoriety. The public regarded their tales as a form of entertainment rather than as a threat, and in time most of these legends were forgotten. The story of David E. George, however, would be different. This tale had a gifted publicist keeping it alive.

Attorney Finis L. Bates was living in Memphis when the news of George's suicide reached him. To Bates this was exciting news, indeed. He had been trying to sell a manuscript on the Booth survival story, but so far nobody was interested. Now he wasted no time in heading for Enid. With characteristic fanfare, he telegraphed ahead to announce his arrival.

Everyone in town seemed eager to hear Bates' story. A solemn scene greeted him in the back room of William B. Penniman's undertaking parlor. There, he looked down at the unclaimed corpse of David E. George and confirmed that this man indeed was the assassin of Abraham Lincoln. Bates was sure of this because, as he explained, twenty-six years earlier the

The corpse of David E. George was a longtime attraction at Penniman's undertaking parlor in Enid, Oklahoma. This picture reportedly was taken eleven days after George's death.

same man had confessed his true identity to him. Back then George (or Booth) was living in Granbury, Texas, and was going by the name of John St. Helen. The fugitive had unburdened his soul to Bates under an attorney-client privilege.

The story seemed a bit bizarre at this point, but it quickly got stranger. Bates spread the word that Booth had, in fact, left a hidden fortune.

Dr. Joseph A. Booth, the last of Booth's siblings, had recently passed away, clearing the way for Bates to begin pressing his own claim to the John Wilkes Booth estate.

Then out of nowhere came the claim of a woman from the East Coast, saying that she was Booth's daughter and would take the inheritance herself. Laura Ida Levine had been born in Tennessee seven years after the

The carnival sideshow exhibit featured the mummified remains of a man said to be John Wilkes Booth.

Civil War, and she always believed that John Wilkes Booth was her natural father. She and Bates would tie up the estate for years, arguing over what proved to be an imaginary fortune. In the meantime, it was David E. George who kept center stage. The corpse remained in Penniman's parlor for the next few years—sitting in a chair, his glass eyes open, and a newspaper draped over his lap. People came from all over to marvel at this masterpiece of the embalmer's art. His photograph appeared in an advertisement for Argon embalming fluid, and one local editor even suggested that the cadaver serve as Oklahoma's contribution to the 1904 St. Louis World's Fair.

Late claimants aside, Finis Bates quickly became the leading custodian of the Booth escape legend. In June 1903, he announced that several of Booth's friends and relatives had confirmed the story of his survival. According to a press release, actors Joe Jefferson and Clara Morris both endorsed Bates' tale, based on a photograph of Booth taken in the 1870s. More important was the cooperation of Booth's niece and nephew, who had signed on to the story as well. Junius Booth III admitted he could see a family resemblance in the photo. His half-sister, Blanche Booth, even added a few details of her own, saying that she might have encountered her uncle in Oklahoma during a recent stage tour. Eventually, she signed a contract to go on tour with the corpse! This marked a turning point in escape folklore, as it gave Bates a credibility that no other purveyor of the Booth legends enjoyed.

With John Wilkes Booth back in the headlines, people started dusting off their memories. A Baltimore newspaper quoted one of the pallbearers at Booth's last burial in 1869 as saying that the remains bore no resemblance to the infamous actor. Basil Moxley, according to this report, called the whole proceeding a "mock funeral" staged for the family's benefit. But others remembered things differently, and a spirited debate flared up for several weeks.

Some newspapers exposed cracks in Finis Bates' story, but the publicity didn't hurt him in the least. In 1907, he published a book entitled *The*

Escape and Suicide of John Wilkes Booth, in which he laid out the full story he had kept secret for so long. The book was a hit, going through several editions. Eventually, Bates took his show on the road, leasing his corpse to carnival side shows. There a small admission fee allowed curiosity seekers to view the body of President Lincoln's assassin, "presented for the correction of history."

It's not hard to understand why the public found Bates' tale so believable. The details of Booth's death left unanswered questions, and, as of 1907, government records on the matter were still sealed. The body was moved three times, and nobody could be sure from press accounts whether it had been buried in the penitentiary or dumped into the Potomac River. Moreover, most people mistakenly believed that the government had never paid any of the reward money it had offered for Booth's capture. All of these issues would eventually be resolved. But for now Finis Bates was not interested. The confusion was working in his favor.

That Bates' book drew wide acceptance in its day doesn't speak well of the reading public. The very first sentence of the book should have sent up a red flag: "President Abraham Lincoln was born near Salem, Kentucky. . . ." Lincoln's actual birthplace is quite well known. Yet the author, who claimed to have spared no effort in checking out his facts, missed the mark by about 170 miles. There were numerous other factual errors, but they didn't keep the book from briskly selling. Ultimately, the public bought 70,000 copies of *The Escape and Suicide of John Wilkes Booth*.

In 1920, Bates offered to sell what was now known as the "Booth mummy" to auto tycoon Henry Ford for the museum of Americana he was planning to build in Dearborn, Michigan. Ford assigned one of his lieutenants, Fred L. Black, to investigate the matter. The project kept Black busy for two years. He traveled to Texas and Oklahoma, interviewing all the people he could find who had once known David E. George or John St. Helen. He checked out rumors of other Booth sightings and pored over the documents and photographs that Bates offered as evidence.

Black was skeptical. In Texas, he learned that Bates had indeed known a

This tintype, said to have been given by Booth to Finis Bates, was supposed to be the key piece of evidence that proved Booth was not killed in 1865.

man named John St. Helen. But old-timers in Granbury laughed at the lawyer's description of him. Far from being the refined gentleman whose oratory had dazzled the townsfolk, St. Helen was actually a brutal thug and con man who had lost his voice when his throat was cut in a knife fight. The Booth story was new to everyone in town, but its genesis wasn't surprising: St. Helen was just the type to play such a joke on a greenhorn lawyer.

In one of their interviews, Black asked Bates why he never checked his facts against the trial testimony. Bates replied that he had no idea (even in 1922) that the record was ever made public. In fact, the conspiracy trial transcripts, published by Benn Pitman, had been a best-seller in 1865. They are still the most basic of all sources on the Lincoln case.

In his book, Bates quoted an article from the *Enid Wave* of January 17, 1903: "David E. George . . . maintained on his deathbed to his attendants that he was John Wilkes Booth, and his general appearance closely resembles that of the murderer of Lincoln." The article, as quoted, told of the arrival of George E. Smith, a man "unknown to any one in Oklahoma," who mysteriously showed up in Enid to have a look at the body. Smith spoke evasively of George's secret past, adding, "I think he killed a man in Texas. He may be Booth."

No such article ever appeared in the *Wave*. In fact, the issue of January 17, 1903, lays out a scenario that contradicted every point in the Finis Bates version. According to the *Wave*, there never was a deathbed confession; two men, hearing George's cries, broke into his room just moments before he died. The shadowy Mr. Smith was actually a former neighbor of George's whom he had named as executor in his will. What Smith really said about the deceased was that his old friend had claimed to be a native of Mississippi, and that he had never mentioned anything to him about John Wilkes Booth.

The article Bates quoted really did come from a newspaper, but not one published in Enid. It had appeared in the *Memphis Commercial-Appeal*, Bates' hometown newspaper, more than a week after the story broke.

Many years later, David Rankin Barbee, the reporter who wrote the article, told a Booth researcher that he got the whole story straight from the lips of Finis L. Bates. From the beginning Barbee was intrigued by the tale, and his follow-up research would make him a world-class authority on Booth and the Lincoln assassination.

Fred Black saw signs of deception in all of Bates' work, and in his papers as well. For example, a sworn affidavit about George's death had been altered to include a deathbed confession. The two men who were present claimed only that they found the man in convulsions just before he died. They reported no confession and no unburdening of the soul. But at the bottom of their statement, a suspicious cluster of words crowded into the corner of the page in a darker ink. The phrase "George declaring on his deathbed that he was John Wilkes Booth" was written there in a different hand, scrawled clumsily through the notary seal.

One bit of evidence that Bates relied very heavily upon was a tintype photograph, which he claimed was given to him by Booth in the 1870s. This picture was the only physical

These mummified remains were the centerpiece of the John Wilkes Booth exhibit that was started by Finis Bates and continued into the 1950s.

"proof" that Bates had ever known the fugitive. According to Bates, it showed the distinctive scar Booth had on his right eyebrow. (Bates' source on this was mistaken, but he believed it nevertheless.) There was just one problem with the tintype. Before anyone was allowed to see it, someone had broken it in half—conveniently, right through the face—and Bates could only explain that the right eyebrow looked awfully bad when it could still be seen. Unfortunately for Bates' purposes, he didn't know much about tintypes. They are mirror images, meaning that what he thought to be the left brow was actually the right. And, as could plainly be seen, the brow in question was perfectly normal.

On the surface, the Booth legend seemed to have some factual basis. After all, the pallbearer, two actor friends of Booth, and two relatives had also endorsed the story. But as Black pointed out, Bates had ignored some very important points. Basil Moxley, the pallbearer, recanted his story almost immediately, claiming the newspaper had misquoted him. Actors Joe Jefferson and Clara Morris denied that they had ever endorsed any of Bates' nonsense. And the assassin's nephew, Junius Booth III, had been born in 1868—too late to have known his uncle. All of this came out in the press during the 1903 debates, but all of it was brushed aside.

In the end, Black concluded that Bates was wrong about Booth's escape. Bates, he said, had ignored testimony, misquoted witnesses, and even falsified documents in order to support his claims. Black published his findings in a series of articles for the *Dearborn Independent*. Eventually he completed an enormous manuscript on the Booth escape legend, but it was never published. Henry Ford wanted nothing further to do with the matter. When Bates died in November 1923, the leathery old corpse was still lying in his garage.

Eight years later, the "John Wilkes Booth mummy" again became the focus of national attention when its new owner hired a team of doctors to perform a scientific evaluation of it for the Chicago Press Club. By comparing the marks and scars on the body with those Booth was "known" to have had, six doctors concluded that the specimen in question was indeed the corpse of Lincoln's killer. Of course, the list of scars came from what they considered the best available source—*The Escape and Suicide of John Wilkes Booth*. Nobody seemed to notice that.

Those scars had always been central to the case. In 1865, the War

Department took great pains to learn how they might identify Booth beyond any doubt. The basic description—five feet, eight inches tall; dark hair "inclined to curl;" and a large, black mustache—fit so many people that hundreds of men were arrested in the days following the assassination. But Henry Clay Young, Booth's actor friend from Cincinnati, described his distinguishing marks in detail: several scars about the chest and another "made by a lady" near one of his armpits. Young said that Booth had been cut on the forehead, close to the hair line, during a stage fight. Of greatest importance, Young confirmed what others had already reported: that Booth's initials were tattooed on the back of his left hand, near the thumb, in India ink.

There was even more. Booth's former manager, Matthew Canning, had once accidentally shot Booth "in the rear" with a revolver. In 1863, Canning had seen Dr. John F. May remove a fibroid tumor from the back of his neck. That operation left a horrible scar. And, of course, the government learned from Dr. Samuel Mudd that Booth had broken a small bone in his left leg on the night of the assassination.

These marks—and a scarred *eyelid*—were all on record in 1865. But Finis Bates knew of only three distinguishing features: a deformed right thumb, smashed in a piece of stage machinery; a scarred right eyebrow, cut in a Cleveland stage fight; and a broken *right* leg. These were the only features sought in the 1931 examination of the mummy, and of course, the body had them all.

There is an old saying that bad men never die. Certainly the matter of America's greatest villain has never been put to rest. The debate has grown even more in recent years, thanks to the 1977 Sunn Classics film, *The Lincoln Conspiracy*, and a 1991 production of NBC-TV's *Unsolved Mysteries*.

Sunn Pictures claimed that the man who died at Garrett's farm was not Booth, but Captain James W. Boyd of the 7th Tennessee Cavalry. Basic research proved that this was impossible. Boyd, six feet tall with gray hair and blue eyes, could hardly have been mistaken for the shorter, black-haired Booth. Moreover, Boyd's death on January 1, 1866, was the most sensational murder case Jackson, Tennessee, had ever seen. When all this was documented in *Civil War Times Illustrated*, Sunn's credibility took a direct hit. Still, the escape theory lived on.

Later, the popular television series *Unsolved Mysteries* aired a dramatization of Booth's survival. The program featured Nathaniel Orlowek and Arthur Ben Chitty, who in numerous press interviews over the years insisted that Booth must have escaped. Encouraged by the public response to their story, Orlowek and Chitty petitioned the courts to allow an exhumation of the remains buried in the Booth family lot. They wanted to determine, through physical inspection, whether it was really John Wilkes Booth who rested there. The management of Green Mount Cemetery opposed the digging. In 1995 the matter was heard in the Baltimore circuit court. By then Orlowek and Chitty had been stricken from the suit and replaced by two Booth relatives.

The Booth family monument in Green Mount Cemetery, Baltimore. Cemetery officials went to court in 1995 to prevent the exhumation of John Wilkes Booth from this lot.

Most versions of the Booth escape theory draw heavily from Finis Bates, and the Baltimore court petition was no exception. At the core of the petitioners' case was the belief that the man who died in Booth's place had not been fully identified. The inquest was limited to people who had barely known the assassin, they said, and even they were reluctant to identify the body with certainty. What troubled those witnesses, according to the legend, was that the corpse in front of them had red hair and freckles. Soldiers who were present at Garrett's farm had also told of shooting a red-haired man, but none of them had mentioned that until the 1920s. This was odd. But according to the petitioners, strict orders and a huge reward check had guaranteed their silence until then.

Green Mount Cemetery called several assassination experts to the stand. All argued that Bates and folklore are simply not believable. Bates' book was largely a fabrication, they testified, while the "red hair" story was refuted by known samples of hair taken from the corpse. They pointed out that all three men who claimed to have seen the "mistake" at Garrett's farm were not actually there, according to their service records. None of the survival stories is supported by physical evidence, except for Bates' broken tintype and an 1872 application for a marriage license. Strangely, "Booth" used his real name here, but he misspelled it. Finally, the experts emphasized that dozens of people, including reporters and relatives, saw the body up close before it was buried.

The Baltimore hearings were the first official test of the theory that Booth was not killed in 1865. Judge Joseph H.H. Kaplan offered his own observations on the carnival mummy, saying that it didn't much resemble Booth. According to trial testimony, this cadaver could not possibly be that of Lincoln's killer. Booth had lustrous dark eyes, most often described as "black." He was extremely bowlegged, was of average height, and had a scar on his neck and the initials "J.W.B." tattooed on his hand. By contrast, the corpse was that of a tall man with deep blue eyes (later replaced by glass) and perfectly straight legs. He had no scar and no tattoo.

After five days of testimony, Judge Kaplan ruled that the petitioners had shown no reason to doubt the traditional story of Booth's death. He rejected their argument that the controversy itself was reason enough to dig up the remains. In handing down his decision, the judge made one point that had been overlooked or misstated in the case: science could have done very little to resolve the matter anyway. The petition had asked for a chance "to determine age, sex, race, stature, body build and the presence of any skeletal injuries. . .," most of which were not at issue. More conclusive tests, such as DNA typing, were not feasible for Booth, who had no confirmed descendants. And so, the anthropologists would have looked over the remains in search of identifying marks that, in all likelihood, were still going to be in dispute.

In reporting the Baltimore hearings, newspapers throughout the world called Judge Kaplan's decision an unfortunate obstacle to learning the truth. But science has often been applied to history in recent years—the exhumations of Zachary Taylor and Lee Harvey Oswald, for example— and it still never seems to quiet the doubters. In the case of John Wilkes Booth, historical research still promises to settle the matter, if anything can.

The progress has already begun. Forthcoming books and documentaries are throwing new light on the topic, eliminating a number of mysteries. For example, research now shows that the 1931 examination of the "Booth mummy" was actually performed by eight men, not six. It turns out that two of them refused to put their names on the final report. Research also suggests that the centerpiece of the John Wilkes Booth carnival exhibit was actually the corpse of an anonymous derelict and not of David E. George.

George himself was no man of mystery. Years after his 1903 suicide, an investigator named George Rainey learned that the deceased had left behind an insurance application. The man had given his name on the form as David Elihu George, house painter and architect, who was born June 14, 1844, near French Camp, Mississippi. Rainey researched the story, and it all seemed to check out. He even spoke with the family that George had abandoned so many years before.

So the mysteries fall, but the Booth legend lives on. Ask anyone in Enid or Granbury today, and they can surely tell you a thing or two about John Wilkes Booth's escape. So can the people of Williamstown, Kentucky; Fayetteville, Tennessee; and Guntown, Mississippi; among others. They all have Booth stories of their own. While the physical proof may be lacking, these legends are never without the sense of mystery and wonder that make American folklore such a fascinating study.

Michael W. Kauffman of Chesapeake Beach, Maryland, has been research-ing the life of John Wilkes Booth for nearly thirty years. In addition to regularly conducting guided tours of Booth's escape route, he has con-tributed articles to American Heritage *and* Civil War Times *and edited the memoirs of Lincoln conspirator Samuel Arnold.*

✥ 5 ✥

The Trial of the Century

THOSE AMERICANS LOYAL TO THE UNION EXPERIENCED a rapid succession of mood swings in the spring of 1865. There was the jubilation over Lee's surrender on April 9, the horror of Lincoln's assassination five days later, the deep satisfaction over his assassin's capture and death on April 26, the extended sorrow of the president's whistlestop funeral tour, and then the ineffable sense of loss that followed his burial on May 4. David Davis, a Supreme Court justice and the president's close friend, spoke for most people in the North when he said: "I shall never become reconciled to Lincoln's death or the manner of it." As the melodrama of the assassination continued through the spring and into summer with the conspiracy trial of several of Booth's accomplices, the collective mood shifted once again—this time to a desire for revenge.

Pudgy, bearded, brusque, and loudly indignant, Edwin Stanton displayed the look and thunderous self-righteousness of an Old Testament prophet. When the tireless and abrasive secretary of war died on Christmas Eve four years later, worn out at the relatively young age of fifty-five, the *Chicago Tribune* eulogized: "While the president jested, the secretary of state gave dinners, and the secretary of the treasury had ambitions for himself, Stanton was the one man alive to the fact that bloody rebellion was to be gashed, stabbed, fought, and humiliated."

Stanton brought that same tough single-mindedness to the task of bringing Booth and his accomplices to justice, though he always considered them mere

Lewis Powell, alias "Paine." Sullen, silent, and powerful, the most enigmatic of the conspirators stands under guard shortly after his arrest.

puppets. From the very beginning he made it clear who he thought pulled the strings: Jefferson Davis and the Confederate high command. This was the same pack of criminals, he

Michael O'Laughlen (left) and Edward Spangler in manacles aboard the Montauk.

charged, that had planned "the disorganization of the North by infernal plots," including arson, germ warfare, the poisoning of water supplies, and the deliberate starvation of tens of thousands of Union prisoners.

Lincoln's death had struck a chord deeper than most people realized in Stanton, who in the past had reacted peculiarly to encounters with the grim reaper. As a young man studying law in Ohio, he had once dug up the grave of a woman who he refused to believe had suddenly succumbed to cholera. When his little daughter died, he had her body exhumed and kept her cremated ashes inside his room for two years. When his wife died, he had dressed her over and over again in her bridal gown until she was buried; afterward he spent nights wandering around the house, calling out her name. After the assassinatic he kept the president's blood-soaked rocking chair inside his office at the War Department—a morbid reminder of what rebellion had wrought. Stanton and most of the North were after vengeance, not punishment.

The government's dragnet resulted in hundreds of men and women being thrown into prison in the first few weeks after the assassination, often for the flimsiest of reasons. Many remained in custody without charges for months, including those who had been cleared as suspects but were needed as witnesses in the upcoming trial.

Of the eight people who Stanton ultimately charged with conspiracy to kill the president, all but three were picked up on the Monday after the killing. Spangler was picked up at his Washington boardinghouse. Arnold, implicated by a letter found in Booth's hotel room, and O'Laughlen also were easily apprehended. That evening a party of detectives and soldiers visited Mary Surratt, whose boarding house had been closely watched in hopes of nabbing her son, John. As the premises were being searched, a disheveled-looking young man suddenly appeared, carrying a large pick over one shoulder and claiming to be a laborer. Mrs. Surratt was asked if she knew

Under cover of darkness and flanked by rows of armed soldiers, the conspirators, hooded and manacled, are moved from ironclads to the Old Penitentiary. There they will stand trial for the death of the president.

this person, to which she responded, "Before God, I never saw him before."

Although they wouldn't know it until they brought him back to headquarters, authorities had nabbed Lewis Powell. Since being abandoned by David Herold following his attack on Secretary of State Seward, he had been hiding in a tree for most of the last two days. Tired, hungry, and desperate, he had

Brigadier General Joseph Holt (left) was judge advocate of the army. President Johnson appointed Holt to be judge advocate and recorder of the military commission that tried the conspirators. Other members of the commission included Brigadier General Robert S. Foster, Brevet Colonel H.L. Burnett, and Brevet Colonel C.H. Tompkins, who served as one of two assistant judge advocates.

dared to visit the only persons he knew in the city. Now he and Mrs. Surratt, who previously had not been a suspect, were taken into custody.

Three days later, on Thursday, April 20, an informer led soldiers to George Atzerodt, who was staying at his cousin's house near Barnsville, Maryland. By the following Thursday, April 27, the last two conspirators Stanton judged guilty enough to go on trial, Dr. Samuel Mudd and David Herold, also were in government hands.

Having winnowed hundreds of suspects down to eight alleged assassins—Spangler, Arnold, O'Laughlen, Atzerodt, Mrs. Surratt, Powell, Dr. Mudd, and Herold—Stanton then devised a cruelly imaginative captivity. Each was fitted with a heavy, padded canvas hood that was worn day and night. There were no eye or ear holes, only a small opening for eating. In addition, a pad of thick cotton was placed over each closed eye. The idea was to prevent any communication among the accused, but the effect of this suffocating, claustrophobic tor-

Major General Lew Wallace, seated at right, was a member of the military court that tried the conspirators. A genuine Union hero, he had helped save Cincinnati and Washington from being captured. Despite his noteworthy military and public careers, Wallace is best remembered today for his 1880 novel, Ben Hur. Joining Wallace in this studio portrait are (from left) fellow commissioners Brigadier General T.M. Harris, Major General David Hunter, Brevet Major General August V. Kautz, Brevet Brigadier General James A. Ekin, and John A. Bingham, who was the other assistant judge advocate.

ture was to almost drive some of the conspirators crazy. Every male prisoner wore at all times wrist irons and anklets, each weighed down with a seventy-five-pound iron ball. Although Mrs. Surratt was spared the hood treatment and her feet were simply chained together, she, too, was not allowed to bathe or wash at any time during her incarceration.

On the night of April 29, the eight were transferred from their below-deck berths on the gunboats *Montauk* and *Saugus* and put into individual cells at the Old Penitentiary Building at the Washington Arsenal. There, inside an improvised courtroom on the third floor, they would have their fates decided by a military tribunal.

Normally, the accused could have expected a civil trial. But Andrew Johnson—sworn in as seventeenth president upon Lincoln's death—had concluded upon the advice of Attorney General James Speed that, because the commander in chief had been assassinated during the time of war, a military trial was perfectly legal and proper. Johnson worried that a civil court would be overly concerned with "technicalities of constitutional law, pedantic adherence to the rules of evidence, or a reasonable doubt." Major General David Hunter served as president of the twelve-man commission charged with trying the accused. Brigadier General Joseph Holt acted as judge advocate and recorder, assisted by judge advocates John A. Bingham and H.L. Burnett. The rest of the tribunal consisted of seven generals and a colonel.

The panel convened for the first time on May 9. The trial would last until the end of June. Under the "common law of war," no spectators were allowed inside the courtroom. But Americans vicariously shared in the spectacle by hungrily devouring the millions of words and countless etchings that appeared in newspapers and magazines during the course of the trial—a trial whose standards of fairness, legality, and impartiality remain highly questionable. Throughout the proceedings the accused sat on a raised platform at the rear of the courtroom. Per Stanton's orders, they were not allowed to testify or to even confer with their lawyers inside their cells. One of the court-appointed defense attorneys, Colonel William Doster, later described the trial as "a contest in which a few lawyers were on one side, and the whole United States on the other—a case in which, of course, the verdict was known beforehand."

Three hundred and forty witnesses took the stand. Especially inflammatory was the testimony of a pair of Union spies, Richard Montgomery and Richard Conover, and Dr. James B.

Mary Surratt and her Washington boardinghouse.

Merritt, a member of the large Southern colony in Canada. They collectively described a plot that linked conspirators, Confederate agents in Canada, and the Rebel government in Richmond. Additional prosecution witnesses buttressed the prosecution's claim that Jefferson Davis's finger had, in effect, been on the trigger of Booth's derringer. There was no hard evidence offered, only hearsay—and perjured testimony, if one believed the numerous published letters and affidavits that discredited Montgomery, Conover, and Merritt as impostors. It was true that Conover—a newspaperman whose real name was Charles Dunham—was a notorious fabricator; that Montgomery had served time for robbery; and that Merritt had received $6,000 from the federal government for his story.

But in the supercharged atmosphere, the tribunal was ready to accept even the most dubious testimony. The public was left to judge the evidence for itself. "It is either overwhelmingly conclusive of the complicity of the Confederate leaders in the assassination conspiracy," summarized the *New York Times*, "or it is an unmitigated lie from beginning to end."

The cases against Powell, Herold, and Atzerodt really didn't need much help. Their guilt was clearly established. Powell was positively identified as the man who had attacked the secretary of state, Herold had been caught with Booth, and Atzerodt admitted to his aborted plan to kill the vice president.

The prosecution's case against the other defendants was more problematic. The only incriminating evidence against Spangler came from a coworker. Jacob Ritterspaugh testified that as Booth ran out of the theater on the night of the assassination, Spangler had hit him in the face with the back of his hand and warned, "Don't say which way he went." Continued Ritterspaugh: "I asked him what he meant by slapping me in the mouth, and he said, 'For God's sake, shut up,' and that was the last he said." Spangler would be found not guilty of the charge of conspiracy, but Ritterspaugh's statement was enough to get him convicted of the lesser charge of aiding and abetting Booth.

Booth's diary was never entered into evidence. Its contents were not generally known at the time, which is how Stanton preferred it. He knew that the disclosure of certain passages would have cast the assassination as a spur-of-the-moment decision by Booth, rather than the end result of an elaborate Confederate conspiracy. It would have harmed the government's case against Arnold, O'Laughlen, Dr. Mudd, and Mrs. Surratt, all of whom were ultimately convicted of having conspired to murder. It certainly would have created reasonable doubt about Mrs. Surratt and undoubtedly saved her from the gallows.

As the days grew warmer in Washington and the crowded courtroom became unbearably stuffy, most of the media attention centered on two defendants: Mrs. Surratt and Powell. The forty-five-year-old widow dressed entirely in black, her thinning but still attractive face hidden behind a heavy veil and a palm-leaf fan. Despite the season, she wore black mittens. As

The Surratt Tavern, first stop on Booth's escape route, circa 1901. Today it houses the Surratt Society, a nonpartisan organization dedicated to researching all aspects of the assassination.

Americans read of the character witnesses who spoke of her kindly Christian nature and of the loving daughter who resolutely stood by her and of her unseemly confinement, they had to balance a sense of sympathy against such published characterizations as "brazen," "defiant," and "an Amazonian of undaunted mettle."

"Undaunted mettle" best described the young man who had unwittingly placed her in chains. The world still knew Powell as Lewis Paine (alternately spelled "Payne" by newspapers), the alias he had given authorities when taking the oath of allegiance.

Powell was an enigma. Almost to the very last, he refused to cooperate with defense attorneys. He revealed nothing of his past and nobody from his family visited him. Faced with this biographical vacuum, newspapers felt free to invent all sorts of stories about the "mystery man" of the conspiracy trial. The most outrageous was that he was the illegitimate son of

Jefferson Davis. Resigned to his fate, Powell spent each day with his head leaned back against the wall, coolly looking out over the courtroom, unmoved by all the legalese. Sometimes he stared dreamily out the barred window, his strong good looks in profile. Some of the soldiers assigned to guard him secretly admired him as one of their own. Unlike the undistinguished group of amateurs and stumblebums he was being tried with, he was a seasoned veteran of several campaigns who had carried out a military mission to the best of his ability.

During the trial, held inside Washington's Old Penitentiary, the conspirators sat on a raised platform at the far end of the courtroom.

He conducted himself like a warrior, accepting the consequences of his actions and refusing to complain about his treatment. In the estimation of several guards, it was too bad that he would be hanged like a common criminal instead of facing a firing squad, the more honorable form of execution.

While everybody inside and outside the courtroom understood that Powell had a date with the hangman, the case against Mrs. Surratt was less convincing. She adamantly denied knowing anything about Booth's plot. Much was made of the fact that she claimed not to recognize Powell when he returned to her boarding house three nights after the murder, though it was soon proved that the two knew each other. Why, then, had she lied? In her defense, it was pointed out that it had been dark, Powell had previously worn a disguise in her presence, and she had extremely poor eyesight. That some of the conspirators regularly visited her boarding house was not a hanging offense. Neither was the fact that she was was strongly sympathetic to the South or that she had operated a suspected safe house for Confederate agents.

However, one of her boarders, Louis J. Weichmann, provided devastating testimony. The twenty-three-year-old government clerk, a former schoolmate of John Surratt who had practically been adopted by his mother, claimed Mrs. Surratt had met with Booth on April 14. He also backed up the testimony of John Lloyd, who tended Surratt's tavern while she was in Washington. Lloyd said that on the day of the assassination, Mrs. Surratt stopped by the tavern and asked him if the hidden "shooting irons" were ready to be picked up that evening. Although Lloyd admitted to being "right smart in liquor" by the time two men did come by, he identified the riders as Booth and Herold. He also repeated Booth's comment just before they rode off: "I am pretty sure we have assassinated the president and Secretary Seward."

Lloyd was extremely fortunate that he wasn't prosecuted for assisting Booth and Herold in their flight and for initially lying about their identities to investigators. Instead, he was used very effectively as a witness for the prosecution. *Too* effectively, claimed critics, who accused Stanton of threatening to put Lloyd and Weichmann on trial for their lives if they didn't give perjured testimony. For his part, Weichmann years later wrote a deathbed letter affirming that everything he had testified to in the trial was true.

Dr. Mudd wasn't as lucky as Lloyd. Like the tavernkeeper, the gentleman physician had also aided the fugitives and then exhibited a selective memory. In his case, these actions clinched his conviction. Nobody on the tribunal believed that he didn't know whose leg he had set in the early morning hours of April 15.

★

All of the defendants except one were convicted of conspiracy; Spangler was judged guilty of aiding Booth's escape. Then commission members gathered to determine sentencing. They voted life imprisonment at hard labor for Arnold, O'Laughlen, and Mudd, and six years at hard labor for Spangler. To no one's surprise, Powell, Atzerodt, and Herold received the death penalty. So did Mrs. Surratt, though the commission attached a recommendation to its findings asking that she be spared on account of her age and sex. They recommended instead that her sentence be changed to life imprisonment.

The commission's findings were ready to be reviewed by President Johnson on June 30, but illness kept Johnson from looking at the report until July 5. Even then he didn't bother to read it; he simply had General Holt give him a summary. Satisfied that justice had been done, Johnson signed the orders sending half of the conspirators to prison and the other half to the scaffold.

The condemned were read their sentences inside their cells the following morning by General Winfield Scott Hancock, commander of the military district, and General John Hartranft, who was responsible for guarding the prisoners. The four conspirators who were spared the noose were kept in suspense until after the hangings. Unlike cases tried in civil courts, military courts allowed no appeals, so justice figured to be swift. Johnson ordered the hangings to be carried out the next day, July 7. Captain Christian Rath would serve as executioner, overseeing the construction and testing of the scaffold and the digging of the graves.

While Powell took the news in stride and Herold and Atzerodt appeared uncomprehending, Mrs. Surratt wept uncontrollably. Between sobs, she professed her innocence to her lawyers and confessors. Beyond the question of her guilt was the issue of her capital punishment. No woman had ever been executed by the government. While ministers and family members visited the doomed inside their cells, consoling them and preparing them for the hereafter, hasty attempts were made to spare this churchgoing woman. Regardless of how one judged her, few people thought that she would actually be hanged. Two Catholic priests kept her company as the appointed hour neared and no word of clemency arrived.

Soldiers came for the condemned early the following afternoon. July 7, 1865, was a wickedly hot day—perfect weather,
thought some of the more stonehearted in attendance, for dis-
patching four murderers to hell. The temperature was
hovering around 100 degrees as the prisoners, flanked by
guards and accompanied by ministers, were led across the sun-
baked yard. They could not help but see the freshly dug graves
and carpentered pine coffins awaiting them just a few yards to
the side of the scaffold. Nonetheless, Powell, cool as a cucum-
ber, playfully snatched the new straw hat off an officer and
placed it atop his own bare head as the doomed climbed the
traditional thirteen steps to the gallows platform.

Soldiers lined the top of the twenty-foot-high prison walls.
Most of the two thousand sightseers who came from near and

far in hopes of witnessing the hangings were out of luck. Only
one hundred tickets were issued to civilian spectators. The rest
of the curious and the ghoulish stood outside the walls and
occupied themselves with drinking lemonade and discussing
the chances of Mary Surratt receiving a last-minute reprieve.

It never came. Earlier that day, President Johnson had
refused to see her hysterically weeping daughter and was
unmoved by a personal appeal from Stephen Douglas's widow.
An emergency writ of habeas corpus, signed by a supreme
court justice of the District of Columbia and hurried to
General Hancock, was nullified by Johnson, who cited the special circumstances of the case. The executions would go on as
planned.

Umbrellas were held over the accused as they sat on chairs in

*David Herold and Lewis Powell
spent the last hours before their executions in dramatically different
fashion. While Herold was com-
forted by his mother and several
sobbing sisters, Powell sat alone in
his cell, knowing no family member
would be able to arrive from Florida
in time.*

The prison yard at the Washington Arsenal, July 7, 1865. On a scorching summer day, four conspirators are readied for hanging. From left to right, the doomed are Mary Surratt, Lewis Powell, David Herold, and George Atzerodt.

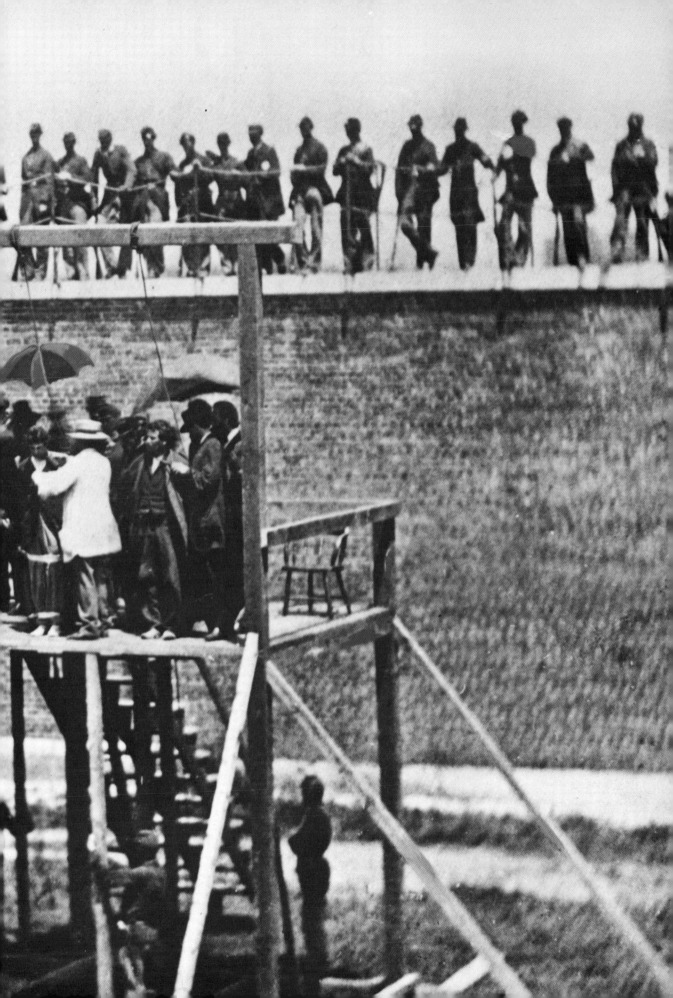

the blazing sun and, attended to by ministers, listened to General Hartranft read the execution order. Mrs. Surratt repeatedly kissed a crucifix. Then they stood to have their arms and legs bound. Next, hoods were placed over their heads and Captain Rath adjusted the nooses around their necks. Except for Powell, who stood straight and tall and conversed easily throughout, all of the conspirators were weak-kneed and frightened by what was to take place. "Don't let me fall," Mrs. Surratt mumbled inside her bag. Just before General Hancock clapped his hands twice to signal the drop, Atzerodt called out: "Good-bye, gentlemen! May we all meet in the other world!"

The hinged floor of the platform suddenly swung open, and the conspirators dropped five feet before Captain Rath's methodically braided nooses violently arrested their fall. Mrs. Surratt died instantly, followed by Atzerodt. It took several minutes for Powell, whose muscular neck did not snap, to strangle. Meanwhile, Herold jerked his body up and down in such a way as to relieve the weight on his neck. But he quickly tired and soon he, too, was dead. It was about two o'clock when Alexander Gardner took one last photograph of the limp, slightly twirling bodies. Then they were brought down and buried, hoods and all, after which Captain Rath began sawing the scaffold into pieces for the benefit of souvenir hunters.

★

The hangings may have satisfied the widespread desire for revenge, but justice was far from perfect. Thomas A. Jones, who along with his stepbrother, Samuel Cox, had kept Booth and Herold hidden for a week inside Zekiah Swamp, never came to trial. Neither did the three young Confederates who guided the fugitives to Garrett's farm. (One, however, paid a price for his betrayal of Booth and Herold. Willie Jett, the young man who had disclosed their whereabouts to detectives, would be ostracized by his neighbors as a traitor for the rest of his life.) Others involved in various other ways escaped prosecution.

Old wounds were ripped open by the assassination and trial. Out the window went Lincoln's policy of mercy for the defeated South, as radical members of Congress followed

Stanton's lead in reacting emotionally, rather than rationally, to the issue of Reconstruction. Military rule was instituted in the former Confederacy and blacks were enfranchised, putting proud Southerners in humiliating daily contact with Yankees and ex-slaves. Official corruption and individual abuses abounded as the North halfheartedly tried to help the South rebuild.

The person Stanton most dearly wanted to see dangling at the end of a rope was Jefferson Davis, who had been captured near Irwinville, Georgia, on the first full day of the conspiracy trial. The president of the Confederacy languished inside a federal prison for two years while Stanton tried to build a capital case on the charge of treason. Although Henry Wirz, commandant of the notorious prison camp in Andersonville, Georgia, was executed, all other high-ranking Confederate military and political leaders were soon released from jail and had their civil rights and U.S. citizenship restored. Davis, released on bail in 1867, lived another twenty-two years on a friend's plantation in Mississippi, steadfastly refusing to petition for official amnesty.

President Johnson, advocate of a more moderate approach to Reconstruction, ultimately was impeached, a prosecution set in motion by his daring to dismiss the meddlesome Stanton. In the trial that followed, Johnson missed being convicted by a single vote. Only then did Stanton, who had refused to leave his barricaded War Department office, resign.

The ghost of Mary Surratt was resurrected during Johnson's embattled presidency. Johnson, who had to fend off spurious allegations that he had somehow been involved with the assassination (Who else stood to benefit from Lincoln's death? went the argument), found himself publicly defending his signing of Mrs. Surratt's death sentence. This happened after the contents of Booth's diary came to light during the trial of John Surratt in 1867. The disclosure seriously damaged the reputation of Stanton, who was now seen by some to have railroaded the poor woman. It was said that she had originally been arrested in hopes of drawing her son out of hiding. He had failed to materialize, so his mother was tried, convicted, and executed as a surrogate.

Regarding her sentence, Johnson claimed that he'd been

given no choice in the matter. He insisted that he had not seen the recommendation for clemency attached to the commission's findings and that General Holt, upon questioning of the punishment, had not informed him of his options. Holt responded that Johnson had not only seen and rejected the recommendation, he'd said something to the effect that her boarding house was the nest in which the plot was hatched.

From that point on the hanging of Mary Surratt was considered by many to be a gross miscarriage of justice. For years to come there remained a reasonable doubt over her guilt.

Then came the discovery of George Atzerodt's written confession one day in 1977. Taken inside his cell on May 1, 1865, and subsequently lost, it had turned up in the papers of his counsel, Colonal Doster. Ironically, it was discovered by a member of the Surratt Society, a group of nonpartisan assassination buffs whose headquarters is the restored tavern of Mary Surratt.

The document contained a simple but damning revelation, one that in the haste and confusion of the trial had been overlooked by prosecutors. On the day of the assassination, said Atzerodt, "Booth told me that Mrs. Surratt went to Surrattsville to get out the guns which had been taken to that place by Herold."

Atzerodt's long-lost confession confirmed what the suspected perjurers, John Lloyd and Louis Weichmann, had testified to in court and vindicated the actions of those two old foes, Johnson and Stanton. For all of her tears and denials, Mary Surratt had indeed willingly taken part in the plot to kill the president. It had taken 112 years, but finally one of the biggest controversies of the "trial of the century" was put to rest.

Hoods fitted and nooses adjusted, the traps were released, and the conspirators dropped to their deaths. They hanged a full half-hour while a crowd outside the prison walls celebrated with lemonade and cakes.

Unlocking the Mystery of Lewis Powell

⇥ BY BETTY OWNSBEY ⇤

EVERYONE IS FAMILIAR with the role played by John Wilkes Booth in the murder of President Lincoln. A lesser known but equally intriguing figure in the drama was Lewis Thornton Powell, the twenty-year-old strongman who went by the alias "Lewis Paine."

During the conspiracy trial the press dubbed the close-mouthed Confederate veteran "The Mystery Man" and speculated wildly about his past. Variously described as "an uneducated dullard," "a murderous cutthroat," and "a hired villain," the would-be assassin of Secretary of State William H. Seward turns out to have been a complex, yet very human, individual. If contemporary sources are to be believed, Powell was a personable young man, gentlemanly and intelligent. Certainly he exhibited considerable courage and class when it came time for several of the conspirators to be fitted for the noose.

Powell was born April 22, 1844, in Randolph County, Alabama, the youngest surviving boy in a family of nine children. His father was a Baptist clergyman, schoolmaster, and gentleman farmer; his second cousin was John Brown Gordon of Georgia, who became one of the South's finest generals during the war.

The family moved to Georgia and then Florida. Powell, educated by his father, was the product of a strict religious upbringing. Family and friends considered him a sensitive and thoughtfully reserved boy. His nickname, "Doc," stemmed from his habit of bringing home and caring for stray animals. His favorite childhood pastime was fishing.

The strapping youngster had aspirations to the ministry when the war broke out in 1861. "Secession fever" changed his career plans. Barely seventeen, two years below the minimum enlistment age, Powell and his best friend from a neighboring farm, Samuel Mitchell, traveled to the township of Live Oak. There they fibbed to the recruiting officer and were enlisted into the 2nd Florida Infantry. Rev. Powell discovered the ruse, but ultimately gave his permission for the boy to join his older brothers, George and Oliver, in uniform.

Powell nearly didn't make it to the front. He was almost immediately stricken with a case of measles so severe that a message was sent to his mother that he was dying. The crisis passed and the weakened soldier joined his outfit outside of Richmond in September 1861. It didn't take long for Powell to become a seasoned veteran. His baptism of fire was at the siege of Yorktown, followed by action in the battles of Seven Pines, Gaines Mill, and Antietam. According to an 1887 article in the *Washington Post*, army life "caused him to fall from piety, but he did not become a prey to drink, that arch enemy to many soldiers. He did become rather fond of cards. He grew tall, well proportioned and fine looking, and his fearless bearing in time of battle was particularly admired. He warmed up as the fight raged and was ever eager to press forward."

Lewis Thornton Powell at fifteen, prior to joining the Confederate army.

Life in the field hardened the clergyman's son, who also looked for ways to while away the weeks of boredom between actions. One comrade remembered him as a "happy boy full of fun and frolic." On one occasion, while on a short leave of absence, the mischievous private took down a pair of pantaloons in front of a store, folded them, walked in, and sold them to the original owner. Another time Powell sent a shopkeeper in hot pursuit of an innocent passerby while he and a friend helped themselves to what they wanted in the store.

Powell, alias Paine, dressed as he looked the night he attacked Seward.

However, Powell could also be "hot headed," it was remembered. There was the time when he lost his hair-trigger temper during a game of quoits and beat his opponent with one of the iron rings. His determination also attracted attention. One recorded episode described his punishment for "gross neglect of his rifle." Powell was sentenced to "mark time between bayonets several days. . . . [The captain] in crossing the camp suddenly came upon the execution of the punishment. The culprit was stepping away hard while the perspiration was running down his face in streams; but instead of 'sulking' he smiled so good-naturedly at his captain that the officer had the sentence remitted."

In early 1863, Powell was notified of the death of his brother, Oliver, at the Battle of Murfreesboro, Tennessee. This, and his mistaken belief that his other brother had also been killed in action, stoked his already red-hot hatred of the Union. He fought at Chancellorsville before being wounded on July 2, 1863, at Gettysburg. Shot through the right wrist, he lay on the battlefield all night before being captured by Minnesota troops the following day.

If Gettysburg represented the high tide of the Confederacy, it also turned out to be the pivotal event of Powell's brief life. Admitted to the 12th Army Corps field hospital for treatment, he ultimately was assigned among the walking wounded as a nurse in Old Dorm, a military field hospital located in Gettysburg College. It was here that Powell met Maggie Branson.

Branson, thirteen years older than Powell and of strong Southern sympathies, had come from Baltimore to nurse the Confederate wounded. Powell and Branson became strongly attached to each other. When Powell was transferred to a prison hospital in Baltimore in August 1863, Miss Maggie decided to return home, ostensibly to keep an eye on her young charge.

Powell, possibly aided by Branson, somehow was able to get his hands on a Union soldier's uniform and escape from the hospital in early September. He stopped briefly to pay a social call at the Bransons' Eutaw Street boardinghouse, where he was introduced to Maggie's younger sister, Mary, before heading south through Union lines in search of his Florida regiment. Instead he fell in with the notorious Marylander Harry S. Gilmore and his band of raiders, a command he soon decided was "too rough."

This was an interesting assessment, considering Powell's warrior background, but it does say something about his sense of fair play. Evidently, Gilmore's raiders robbed and mistreated a group of Jewish peddlers, an act Powell denounced. As he told the Branson sisters, he was above such simple thievery. He deserted the command.

Powell subsequently joined Company B of Colonel John S. Mosby's 43rd Virignia Battalion. He would remain with the storied Mosby's Rangers for the next year and a half.

Mosby's guerrillas boarded at various homes scattered throughout the northern Virginia countryside. Like the minutemen of the American Revolution, they would ride to arms at the first sign of alarm, meeting at a prearranged spot to quickly discuss and then carry out their hit-and-run tactics.

Powell enjoyed the partisan ranger lifestyle. He was remembered by one of Mosby's men as an eager youngster who was always "keyed up for any new sensation . . . a first class fighting man, always ready for any duty, and game." He was highly regarded by the Payne family of Warrenton, Virginia, with whom he boarded while serving with Mosby. The head of the family, General William H. Payne, recalled Powell as a "chivalrous, generous, gallant gentleman" who was very fond of his young children. He also grew enamored with a young Payne cousin, Betty Meredith, whom he began courting.

A rare engraving of the conspiracy trial shows the accused and the military commission trying them.

In January 1865, Powell said good-bye to Meredith and left Mosby's unit. His abrupt departure seemed odd, given his affection for his outfit and Miss Betty. Six months later, inside his cell after being sentenced to death for his part in the Lincoln murder, Powell would confess to his spiritual advisor that during this period he had been working with the Confederate secret service.

Had Powell really been part of a larger conspiracy? The evidence is circumstantial, but I believe he was. According to various sources, he was one of five men hand-picked by Mosby to carry out an order from highly placed Confederate officials (exactly who has never been determined) to abduct—not murder—Lincoln. The idea was to hold him in exchange for Confederate prisoners of war. Four of Mosby's Rangers reportedly decided to back out at the last moment. Only the young and idealistic Powell decided to go through with the venture.

Shortly after leaving Mosby's command, Powell showed up at the Branson boardinghouse, this time as a paying guest. It seems likely that the Bransons were operating a Confederate safe house. Powell blended into the household, accompanying Mary Branson on various social calls when he wasn't involved in his secret-service work. Through the Bransons, he became acquainted with David Preston Parr, a local china merchant and operative. Working as Powell's contact, Parr introduced Powell to a young Confederate courier named John Surratt, Jr., who was working under the orders of Confederate Secretary of War Judah P. Benjamin. It was through Surratt that Powell met a popular actor by the name of John Wilkes Booth.

About the middle of February, Powell journeyed to Washington to pay a call on Surratt. He wasn't in, but he was given a meal and lodging by Surratt's mother, Mary Surratt. Powell gave the widow the information he had for young Surratt and returned to Baltimore the next day. This was Powell's first visit to the Surratt boardinghouse.

In March, Powell got into a fracas with a black maid at the Bransons' boardinghouse, which led to his being brought before Provost Marshal Captain H.B. Smith. He was held two days and then ordered to sign an oath of allegiance to the United States. He was instructed to go north of Philadelphia and stay there for the duration of the war. Curiously, Powell was listed on the docket with the charge of "spy" and not with the original charge of "assault and battery." Had he complied with the terms of the document, he probably would have escaped an early death on the gallows. As it was, he packed his belongings and headed for the Surratt boarding-house. He boarded there for the next week as the "Reverend Dr. Paine," using the alias with which he had signed his oath of allegiance.

The plot to kidnap the president was quite complex. There is good reason to believe that Powell traveled with Surratt and Booth as they met with secret service operatives in Canada and New York. After the plot fizzled around the middle of March, Powell sent a letter to Maggie Branson, telling her that she could write him at a New York hotel, the Revere House. By March 27 he was putting up at the Herndon House at the corner of 9th and F Streets in Washington, through arrangements made with John Surratt. Even as Richmond fell and Lee surrendered the Army of Northern Virginia in early April, Powell and his new companions believed that the South's cause was not yet lost. Powell later stated that, until the day of April 14, 1865, nothing other than the abduction of the president was planned.

Meanwhile, Powell had been making periodic stops by Secretary of State Seward's house on Lafayette Square to flirt with a pretty parlor maid named Margaret Coleman. He also inquired about the secretary's health, as he had been seriously injured in a carriage accident and was bedridden. By the afternoon of the 14th, however, plans had changed. Powell's role was to assassinate Seward, assisted by David Herold, a drugstore clerk who would help him escape through the unfamiliar streets of Washington.

One wonders why Powell, who appears to have been an intelligent person and of a sound moral background, would agree to such an undertaking. He seems to have thought of himself as a Confederate patriot, or so he told a clergyman upon the eve of his execution. He expected no pay, he said, only the gratitude of the Southern people. Misguided youth or not, Powell went through with his plan which, although violent and bloody, failed. Three days later he was arrested at the Surratt House and taken into custody as Lewis Paine.

Young "Paine" impressed his captors with his stoic demeanor while incarcerated, even when subjected to hooding and shackles. Although he was quite upset when first hooded—repeatedly crashing his head against the stone wall in an apparent attempt to bash his brains out—he soon accepted his treatment with little complaint or comment.

Powell maintained Mary Surratt's innocence, to no avail. They left the world, side by side, at the end of a noose.

As the conspiracy trial began in May 1865, Powell was secondary in the public spotlight only to Mary Surratt. The newspapers were full of stories about the impassive young man who sat with his head leaning against the wall, staring defiantly out over the court. The prison guards admired his cool audacity and female spectators were titillated by his dark good looks. Captain Christian Rath, a member of General John Hartranft's staff, found him quite friendly when away from the courtroom. They grew fond of each other, engaging in quoit games in the prison yard and inventing practical jokes to play on each other.

Powell's government-appointed attorney, William E. Doster, knew nothing about the boy and could get nothing out of him. Court-appointed doctors had examined him and described him as slow and unresponsive. Although this could have been a ruse to fool the doctors, it also may have been the result of the traumatic hooding process that had caused the same state of mental confusion noted in another of the accused conspirators, Edman Spangler. Powell's puzzling silence added to his aura of mystery and spurred the press to invent sensational stories about the man known as Lewis Paine. They variously reported that he was a medical student from Baltimore who had gone berserk; that he was one of St. Albin's Raiders from Vermont; and that he was Dan Murray Lee, cousin of General Robert E. Lee. The most spectacular allegation was that he was the illegitimate son of Jefferson Davis, president of the Confederacy.

Doster, with no other obvious way to save his client, decided to offer an insanity plea. Apparently Doster did not consult Powell about this, because when it was first brought up in court, Powell appeared utterly mortified. It didn't matter, as the insanity plea was rejected. It was at this point, with only a couple of weeks left to go in the two-month trial, that Powell finally decided to communicate with his counsel. He admitted his true identity and requested that his father come to Washington to testify in his behalf. Rev. Powell apparently was ill at the time and the notification to come to Washington City did not make its way through the war-torn South in time.

The verdict was handed down on June 30, 1865. Powell was found guilty and was one of four conspirators sentenced to be hanged. The condemned were notified of the sentence on the morning of July 6. Powell, expecting this outcome all along, took the news in stride. He asked only that the Reverend Dr. Augustus Stryker, the Branson family's Episcopal clergyman, come to his aid. However, it wouldn't be until noon of the following day, just one hour before the scheduled execution, that he arrived.

One report stated that Powell also asked that should "two others" arrive, they should be admitted. Powell apparently was thinking of the Branson sisters. They never came. Powell knew there was no way that his family in Florida could possibly make the trip to see him. At the suggestion of prison officials, a local Baptist clergyman, the Reverend Dr. Albram Dunn Gillette, arrived to assist Powell. Gillette, whose own son was Powell's age, stayed with him through the night of July 6–7 and up to the hour of execution.

Rev. Gillette was a complete stranger to Powell, but the condemned opened up and spoke freely to him. He talked of his family, his home, and of his military career, though he remained reserved when speaking about the conspiracy and the participants. He was extremely upset over the fate of Mary Surratt, who had been sentenced to join him on the gallows. He was almost frantic in protesting her innocence to anyone within earshot. According to Powell, the widow knew nothing about the murder plot. Was this the truth or simply chivalry on Powell's part? Many believed Powell's assertions then, and the debate over Surratt's guilt or innocence continues to this day. Powell also claimed that George Atzerodt was innocent of attempted murder.

Captain Rath was the hangman. It was his duty to design and oversee the construction of the scaffold, as well as the making of the nooses and hanging hoods.

Shortly after 1:00 P.M. on July 7, 1865, the death march began. Powell, whose sole visitors had been the two clergymen, was the last to be led out of his cell and onto the scaffold. He was seated next to Surratt. Unlike his doomed co-conspirators, he remained calm. After the reading of the execution order, Rev. Gillette advanced to the front of the scaffold to speak in Powell's behalf, thanking the prison officials for their kindness to him. The clergyman then offered a prayer for Powell, which moved the condemned man to tears. It was the first public display of emotion he had shown since his capture. At this point Captain Rath adjusted the noose on Powell's neck, telling him that he wanted him to "die quick."

"You know best, Captain," came the muffled reply from under the hood. "I thank you. Good-bye." Those were Powell's last words.

The drop fell at about 1:25 P.M. Powell, whose neck was not broken, strangled for between five and eight minutes before he died. According to the *New York World*, it "was a dishonored death for a most unsoldierly deed. At least Payne gave to it something of dignity by calmness, modesty, and silence."

The bodies of the four conspirators were buried in the prison yard, at the foot of the scaffold. Within four years all but Powell's were released to their respective families. His remained unclaimed and was subsequently disinterred and reburied in Graceland Cemetery near Georgetown. The cemetery later was subdivided and the grave plots removed. Powell's body was reburied in Holmead Cemetery.

In 1871, Powell's father and brother finally made the journey from Florida to claim his remains. They brought the casket back south as far as North Carolina, at which point the elder Powell fell ill from pneumonia. While he recuperated, his disgraced son was buried on the farm. This temporary solution lasted eight years. Finally, in 1879, Powell was removed to Geneva, Florida, where he was laid to rest beside his mother.

This was when the family made a gruesome discovery: They had been hauling around a headless corpse. Unbeknownst to them, an undertaker had removed Powell's skull when the body was disinterred from the prison grounds in 1869. The skull was given to the Army Medical Museum, which later consigned it to the Smithsonian Institute. It was lost in the stack area until January 1992, when it was discovered packed away with the skulls of several hundred Native Americans. Lewis Powell's skull was positively identified by historians and family members and, after an absence of 125 years, reunited with the rest of his remains in a graveside service in November 1994.

Betty Ownsbey, an engineering draftsman and graphic illustrator in Richmond, Virginia, has spent twenty years researching Lewis Powell's life. She is the author of Alias "Paine": Lewis Thornton Powell, the Mystery Man of the Lincoln Conspiracy.

Apotheosis images of Lincoln frequently showed the martyred president being welcomed into heaven by George Washington.

6

The Aftermath of Madness

T HE FACT THAT LINCOLN WAS SHOT ON GOOD FRIDAY, the same day Jesus Christ had been crucified, fueled his apotheosis after the assassination. On Easter Sunday, 1865—"Black Easter" to millions of mourning Americans—ministers felt free to portray the slain president as an American Christ. One reverend told his flock: "It is no blasphemy against the Son of God and the Savior of men that we declare the fitness of the slaying of the second Father of our Republic on the anniversary of the day on which He was slain. Jesus Christ died for the world, Abraham Lincoln died for his country."

The feeling of loss was particularly keen among freedmen, whose homes would contain pictures of the Great Emancipator well into the next century. "Humanity has lost a firm advocate, our race its Patron Saint, and the good of all the world a fitting object to emulate," wrote one black soldier. The name of Abraham Lincoln, he continued, "will ever be cherished in our hearts, and none will more delight to lisp his name in reverence than the future generations of our people."

In years to follow, the popular image of the martyred Father Abraham would fall in and out of fashion, depending on the mood and needs of the country. The Lincoln mythologized by poet-biographer Carl Sandburg on the eve of the Second World War would not be the same one demonized by "Black Power" activists during the 1960s. Through all the revisionism, interest in the sixteenth president has never waned; in fact, more books have been written about him than any other figure in American history.

His assassin, looking for fame, instead found infamy. To be sure, there were scattered handclaps over his deed, particularly among Lincoln-haters in the South, who considered the president a tyrant and his killer a patriot. But the ovation John Wilkes Booth anticipated never materialized. Even his adoring sister, Asia, who generally wrote and spoke of him with indulgence and affection, admitted to the eternal shame his act had visited upon the family name. A few weeks after his death at Garrett's farm, she penned a letter to her close friend, Jean Anderson.

"The sorrow of his death is very bitter," she confided, "but the disgrace is far heavier—Already people are asserting that it is a political affair—the work of the bloody rebellion—the enthusiastic love of country, etc., but I am afraid to us it will always be a crime."

★

John Surratt.

What of the others involved—some principally, others peripherally—in the tragedy of April 14, 1865?

John Surratt had managed to avoid being tried with the other conspirators by fleeing to Canada, where he was hidden by sympathetic Catholic priests. The fact that he abandoned his mother doesn't speak well for him, though his return would have been of no help, and he undoubtedly believed, as almost everybody did, that the government would never execute a woman.

After the government proved everybody wrong, Surratt sailed, in disguise, to England, then on to Rome, where he enlisted in the Papal Zouaves as "John Watson." He confessed his past to an American member of the guard, who forwarded the information to the U.S. embassy. In November 1866, the Vatican ordered his arrest, but Surratt managed to escape his captors, at one point surviving a blind leap into a twenty-five-foot-deep ravine. He made his way to Naples, where he fast-talked the British consul into believing that he was a Canadian citizen. He secured passage to Alexandria, Egypt, but the fugitive's run from justice ended there with his arrest by the American consul-general.

Surratt was tried for murder in the criminal court of the District of Columbia in the summer of 1867. It was during the two-month-long trial that the contents of Booth's diary first became public knowledge. Surratt's defenders made much of one passage in particular: "April 14, Friday, the Ides: Until today nothing was ever thought of sacrificing to our country's wrongs. For six months we had worked to capture, but our cause being almost lost, something decisive and great must be done. . . ." This proved, said the defense, that the assassination had been a hasty, unilateral decision by Booth. Surratt knew only of a plot to kidnap the president, not to kill him. And in any case, Surratt had been in New York the day of the murder.

The prosecution argued that Booth had written his diary entries after the assassination. Displaying his characteristic blend of chivalry and ego, Booth had hoped to clear his fellow conspirators of blame while simultaneously grabbing sole credit for the murder.

William Seward carried the evidence of Lewis Powell's savage knife attack on his scarred face until his death in 1872.

It didn't help the government's case that the ghost of Mary Surratt was invoked at every opportunity. The jury, split along regional lines, could come to no agreement. Eight jurors were citizens of Virginia, Maryland, or the District of Columbia, and each voted for acquittal. The remaining four were citizens of the North, and each voted for conviction. A mistrial was declared. Authorities pondered a new trial, well aware that jurors would continue to be selected from a region that was strongly sympathetic to the South. Finally, realizing that another hung jury was far more likely than a hanged defendant, they declined to try Surratt a second time.

Having had his fill of adventure, Surratt made a brief, unsuccessful appearance on the lecture circuit before settling into a mundane life as a low-level clerk in Baltimore. He died in 1916, maintaining to the last that he and his mother had nothing to do with Lincoln's death.

The four conspirators sentenced to prison terms arrived at Fort Jefferson on July 15, 1865, after a week at sea. Fort Jefferson, the Alcatraz of its day, sat about one hundred miles off the coast of Florida, in the infamous Dry Tortugas. The prison's most notable feature was a shark-filled moat that surrounded the fort. Guards regularly tested the waters, so to speak, by throwing in live cats. The essence of this barren, sun-

The roundly reviled John Wilkes Booth was portrayed by this post-assassination artist as being in cahoots with the devil. Asia Booth Clarke much preferred to view her murderous older brother as a misguided Southern patriot. Asia, the family historian, wrote biographies of her father and two of her brothers.

baked island hell could be found in the message a previous prisoner had left scrawled on the door of Dr. Mudd's cell: "Leave hope behind who enters here."

Outside of cleaning bricks, prisoners sentenced to hard labor actually did very little work at Fort Jefferson. Escape was not unheard of. Two months into his confinement, Mudd, with the assistance of a crew hand, managed to squirrel himself away on a visiting steamer, though he was recaptured within ten minutes. Inmates found one aspect of their imprisonment particularly oppressive: being guarded by Negro troops. In a letter to his wife, Mudd complained that it was "bad enough to be a prisoner in the hands of white men, your equals under the Constitution," but being constantly watched over by one's inferiors was almost enough to make an inmate want to jump into the moat.

In August 1867, yellow fever broke out at Fort Jefferson. Among its many victims were conspirators Michael O'Laughlen and Samuel Arnold. Mudd attended to both, though O'Laughlen died. After the chief physician also succumbed, Mudd took temporary command of the overcrowded, makeshift medical facilities. His work in controlling the epidemic was brought to the attention of Washington, though the blanket amnesty President Andrew Johnson granted all former Confederates was not extended to those involved in the assassination. By February 1869, however, at which time Johnson was getting ready to leave the White House, the chief executive's mind had changed. He pardoned the three remaining conspirators—Mudd, Arnold, and Edman Spangler—and soon after allowed the graves of Booth and the four hanged conspirators to be exhumed and properly reburied by their families.

Mudd returned to his Maryland home, in time taking in Spangler. The two died eight years apart—the stagehand in 1875, the physician in 1883—with each leaving behind a sworn declaration of his innocence. Thanks to the indefatigable lobbying efforts of descendants, Mudd has since fared better in public memory than any of his fellow inmates. In 1959 a plaque commemorating his role in the yellow fever crisis was installed at Fort Jefferson; in 1973 the State of Michigan passed a resolution declaring his innocence; and in 1979 the doctor was unofficially exonerated by President Jimmy Carter.

Boston Corbett, the trooper credited with killing the man whose leg Mudd set, collected $1,653.85 in reward money, the same amount all other enlisted members of his outfit received. He also got a court-martial for his trouble. Charged with shooting without orders, Corbett saw his actions defended by Lieutenant Doherty—who testified that the defendant was a courageous fellow who had thrice volunteered to personally haul the assassin out of the barn—and commended by Secretary of War Stanton, who announced: "The rebel is dead, the patriot lives—has saved us continued excitement, delay, and expense. The patriot is released."

Ten years later, Corbett was discovered brandishing a pistol at a veterans' reunion in Caldwell, Ohio. According to one eyewitness, Corbett "was always well armed, in self-defense, as he explained, and his experience at Caldwell showed that he had some reason to fear violence. He got into an exciting argument with several men one afternoon over the question as to whether Booth had really been killed at all. Hot words ensued, a rush was made towards Corbett, and in an instant the gleaming barrel of his revolver flashed in the faces of his opponents."

This kind of heavy-handed righteousness was bound to spell trouble for Corbett, who continued to sport a pair of pistols in his new role as assistant doorkeeper of the state capitol in Topeka, Kansas. Friends had gotten Corbett the job after he had failed at farming. After breaking up, at gunpoint, a "blasphemous" mock legislative session conducted by playful clerks and pages, Corbett was hauled off to jail. He was declared insane and placed in a Topeka asylum. He soon escaped—headed, some thought, to Mexico. He was never seen or heard from again.

Thomas "Boston" Corbett. After Providence directed him to shoot Booth, he moved to Kansas, went insane, and disappeared forever.

Actress Jennie Gourlay and her future husband, conductor William Withers, were both in Booth's path as he fled across the Ford Theater stage and into the night. Each had minor moments of glory stolen from them by the murder.

Gourlay, the leading lady of the Ford stock company, was to have starred in a benefit performance of *The Octoroon* the following evening. However, except for a re-enactment of *Our American Cousin* for the War Department during the conspiracy trial—to determine whether it would have been possible for any of the actors to have aided Booth during the course of the production—no play was ever again held at Ford's Theater. The building, first sealed and then bought by the government, was retrofitted for use as the Army Medical Museum. Its most popular display was John Wilkes Booth's shattered vertebrae. In

1893, on the day of Edwin Booth's funeral, the third floor of the building collapsed, killing twenty-two people and injuring sixty-eight others.

Withers had created a special composition, *Honor to Our Soldiers*, for President Lincoln. It originally was intended to be sung by the cast of *Our American Cousin* at an early intermission. Moved back to the end of the Good Friday performance, it was put on hold for 125 years by the unscripted horror of the assassination. Finally, in 1990, Withers' song was performed inside the new Ford's Theater, which had been renovated between 1965 and 1968 and re-opened as a working theater and a National Historic Site. Today its basement holds many relics from the assassination, including Booth's derringer and knife.

Jennie Gourlay.

Gourlay and Withers were just two of about one thousand people present at Ford's Theater the night of the assassination. Each person would, for the rest of his or her days, tell wide-eyed grandchildren and inquisitive reporters a different story of what had happened.

No two eyewitness accounts matched detail for detail. To cite just one of many examples, some people claimed Booth shouted, "The South is avenged!" or, "Revenge for the South!" on stage after shooting the president. Others insisted he declared, "*Sic semper tyrannis!*" At least one member of the audience maintained that Booth's words were "I have done it!" Still others swore they heard the assassin say nothing at all.

Some stories lacked credibility, such as the widely circulated claim of Jacob Soles—sixty-six years after the fact—that he and three other Union soldiers had helped carry the stricken president across the street to the bedroom in which he died. In actuality, to this day nobody knows for sure how Lincoln was transported from the theater to the Petersen House. Was it on a shutter, the box partition, or in somebody's arms? And the number and identities of the people who did the carrying vary widely, depending on the account.

The list of contradictory testimony and conflicting boasts, covering nearly all aspects of the assassination, goes on and on. Seemingly the only point of agreement among all the people

Better late than never: conductor William Withers and his orchestral salute to the victorious Union army, Honor to Our Soldiers.

there that night was that Abraham Lincoln had indeed been shot.

Samuel J. Seymour was just five years old when he and his godmother, Mrs. Goldsborough, took their seats in the balcony opposite Lincoln's box. In 1955, a reporter caught up with Seymour at his daughter's house in Arlington, Virginia, and asked for his recollections of that awful night at Ford's Theater.

Seymour thought hard. It had been ninety years. In the old

fellow's muddied memory the president had been standing when he was shot, despite overwhelming evidence to the contrary.

"There was lots of excitement," he added. "People were hollering and screaming and crying. I began to cry and Mrs. Goldsborough took me out of the theater."

And that was that. A few months later, in early 1956, the last surviving eyewitness to the tragedy died at the age of ninety-six.

★

One aspect of the assassination that is seldom remarked upon is the collective toll suffered by the four occupants of the presidential box on April 14, 1865. All were either murdered or declared insane. The president, of course, was assassinated, leaving Mrs. Lincoln, Major Henry Rathbone, and his fiancee, Clara Harris, to fulfill their own dismal destinies.

Mary Todd Lincoln, an emotionally unstable person to begin with, became wholly "unhinged by the shock," said a good friend. Ordered out of the room where her husband lay dying, she returned for one last look after he expired, then withdrew to her bedroom inside the executive mansion. She stayed there, immobilized, for nearly six weeks, missing all of the services and the funeral train to Springfield. "Why, why was I not taken when my darling husband was called from my side?" she cried over and over.

"Tad's grief at his father's death was as great as the grief of his mother, but her terrible outbursts awed the boy into silence," remembered seamstress Elizabeth Keckley, who was her closest companion during this period. "Sometimes he would throw his arms around her neck, and exclaim, between his broken sobs, 'Don't cry so, Mamma! Don't cry, or you will make me cry, too! You will break my heart!' Mrs. Lincoln could not bear to hear Tad cry, and when he would plead to her not to break his heart, she would calm herself with a great effort, and clasp her child in her arms."

While Mary grieved inconsolably behind closed doors, people strolled in off the street and systematically looted the White House of anything that could be considered a souvenir, including furniture, silverware, bedding, china, and fragments of the drapes and velvet carpeting. When she finally left to make way for President Johnson, some accused the former First Lady of hiding stolen valuables inside her seventy cartons of belongings.

This set the tone for the remaining seventeen years of her life, a period marked by rancor, despair, public humiliation, and a deep slide into melancholia. Mary, who never wore anything but widow's black after the assassination, lashed out irrationally at guard John Parker and President Johnson, accusing both of complicity in the murder. She kept up a running feud with William Herndon, the president's former law partner, and disowned Keckley, after both came out with books that were less than flattering to her.

She became obsessed with money, though on the surface her finances seemed sound. In December 1865, she received a lump-sum payment of $25,000—equal to one year of her husband's salary—from Congress. But she foolishly plunked down most of the money on a Chicago house she couldn't afford and continued to ring up store debts. Her unpopularity made it next to impossible for friends to raise money in her name, such as was commonly done for the widows of generals and politicians. In 1867 she tried to sell her vast wardrobe anonymously through some unscrupulous brokers, a debacle that only earned her widespread ridicule and abuse. She was a "mercenary prostitute," declared one newspaper. "Only my darling Taddie prevents my taking my life," she wrote at this time.

In 1868 she and Tad left the country for Germany. Closed up inside a Frankfurt hotel, she petitioned Congress for a pension while awaiting the settlement of her husband's estate. Within three years word of both arrived, prompting her and Tad's return to the States. In addition to receiving a government pension of $3,000 annually (later raised to $5,000 and supplemented by a $15,000 donation), investment income from her one-third share of Lincoln's $85,000 estate (split evenly with sons Tad and Robert) provided her with another $1,500 to $1,800 a year. She would never want for money, though in her addled state she would always believe herself to be on the brink of poverty.

There was no question that she was emotionally impoverished. On their ocean voyage back to America, Tad caught a chest cold, a condition that worsened as they settled into Robert Lincoln's Chicago mansion. Tad's lungs filled with liquid, making it difficult to breathe and placing a great strain on his heart. He died July 15, 1871, at age eighteen—the third Lincoln son to fail to reach manhood.

The only one of Mary's sons to survive adolescence, Robert, was by now a successful lawyer. In time he would become President James Garfield's secretary of war, minister to England during the Benjamin Harrison administration, and the fabulously rich president of the Pullman Car Company. For all of his money and accomplishments, at his death in 1926 Robert Lincoln would be remembered by some as being as cold as the marble inside his Vermont mansion. This was Mary's view in the years following Tad's death, as her only child worked to have her institutionalized.

By 1875, Robert had become alarmed by his mother's infatuation with spiritualism, her growing dependence on narcotics, and her increasingly erratic behavior. She claimed to have communicated with the dead president at seances, her visions undoubtedly assisted by regular doses of laudanum, chloral hydrate, and opium. She once got into a hotel elevator undressed, convinced that it was a lavatory, and continued to squander large amounts of money on wholesale lots of gloves, handkerchiefs, and other items. She suffered more than ever from migraine headaches; an Indian, she said, was pulling wires through her eyes.

Concerned with his mother's welfare and with his own reputation (as well as with the very real possibility that she would spend his inheritance), Robert successfully petitioned the Cook County Court to have her committed to a private sanitarium near Chicago. Betrayed by her son and now officially a "lunatic" in the

Robert Todd Lincoln.

eyes of the law, Mary tried to commit suicide with an overdose of drugs. She survived the botched attempt and, with the help of friends, was released after four months to the care of her sister, Elizabeth.

Mary ultimately was declared sane in a second trial, after which she again fled to Europe. For three years she stayed in a squalid French hotel, battling arthritis, cursing Robert, gulping bottles of opium-laced "restorative," and seldom venturing out. In 1880, crippled and nearly blind, she returned for good to Elizabeth's Springfield home. There she spent the last two years of her life, the curtains drawn in her bedroom as she busied herself, by candlelight, with her sixty-four trunks of clothes, as if she were getting everything in order for a long journey whose departure date was growing ever more imminent.

Mary Todd Lincoln fell into a coma and died on July 15, 1882, the eleventh anniversary of Tad's death. Her great niece, Mary Edwards Brown, who helped care for her in her final days, remembered the worn wedding band with the message, "Love Is Eternal," inscribed on it. It had been removed because of Mary's badly swollen fingers. "After Aunt Mary died," she recalled, "Mother hunted it up and got it back again on her finger. . . . The newspapers wrote about the ring when she was lying in her coffin in Grandmother's parlor with the wedding lamps lighted, how the ring was Etruscan gold and was shining on her finger and there was a smile on her face."

Major Henry Rathbone recovered from his wounds and married Clara Harris in 1867. The couple moved to Hanover, Germany, where Rathbone served as American consul. Distance, however, could not ease memories of that terrible evening at Ford's Theater nor diminish feelings of personal responsibility. The guilt-wracked officer tortured himself with thoughts of what might have been. If only he had seated himself next to or behind the president, vigilantly keeping guard instead of lounging on the couch, then he would have been in a position to intercept the assassin. In his mind, the entire future flow of history had been affected by his failure to protect Lincoln. The echo of a derringer blast seemed to grow stronger, not fainter, with the passing of time. Plagued by dyspepsia, severe headaches, and spells of deep depression, the brooding Rathbone—like Mary Lincoln—turned to opiate medications for relief. Instead, they helped push him over the edge.

On Christmas Eve, 1883, he accused Clara at gunpoint of planning to take their young children and leave him. Clara, panicking over this latest display of her husband's paranoia, screamed for the nursemaid.

"Louise," she yelled, "there is devilment afoot! Lock the children's door!"

As the maid and the children huddled in horror in a corner of the locked nursery, Rathbone shot and then stabbed Clara. "Henry, let me live!" she shrieked. This was followed by one last cry: "Oh, don't!"

Police arrived to find Clara sprawled on the bed, blood pooling under her lifeless body. Her dazed assailant was on the floor, cowering by the stove. His body was covered with self-inflicted stab wounds, and he was mumbling, "Who could have done this to my darling wife?" He gibbered about people "hidden behind the pictures on the wall." Perhaps one of those haunting images was John Wilkes Booth.

Rathbone was judged criminally insane and spent the rest of his life in a mental institution in Hildescheim, Germany. He died in 1911 during his seventy-fourth year, one more victim of that long-ago night of madness at Ford's Theater.

The Reel Lives of Lincoln and Booth

⇥ BY RICHARD E. SLOAN ⇤

DRAMATISTS HAVE always been fascinated with Abraham Lincoln, whose life and death are tailor-made for the stage, the big screen, and television. For here was a man of humble beginnings who saved the Union and was cut down by an assassin's bullet in his hour of victory. Additional creative fodder can be found in the story of John Wilkes Booth—a matinee idol from a famous family, suddenly transformed by his contemptible deed into an American Judas.

In the stage melodramas of the nineteenth century, Lincoln usually was cast as a kind of country bumpkin, going from scene to scene saying, "That reminds me of a good joke." It was Booth, depicted as the cardboard villain typical of the period, who usually had the lead role. With waxed mustache and flowing cape, he could be counted on to say, "Curses! Foiled again!" or, "Laugh, you old gorilla; your time has come!" In some of these melo-

In his best known performance as Lincoln, The Littlest Rebel *(1935), Frank McGlynn saved the life of Shirley Temple's father, who had wrongly been accused of spying.*

dramas Lincoln's ghost returned to haunt Booth; only then was the president treated with deference.

With the advent of silent films at the turn of the century, Lincoln replaced Booth as the dominant character in dramatizations. These early films usually were fanciful tales in which the president either granted a pardon to a young soldier about to be executed or defended a lad in a mur-

Frank McGlynn as Lincoln is about to get shot in Edison's 1915 silent film, commissioned by the state of Illinois.

der trial. These were based on well-known incidents in Lincoln's life and appealed to both movie makers and movie fans.

A rather primitive 1915 biographical effort, *The Life of Abraham Lincoln*, starred Frank McGlynn in the title role. This landmark work was commissioned by the state of Illinois and produced by Thomas Edison at his Bronx, New York, studio. McGlynn—who would go on to play Lincoln in a number of films and plays—somberly portrayed the president as the patient savior of the nation, who frequently looked to heaven for guidance and inspiration. The film contains a number of brief, stilted tableaux. These include the debates with Stephen A. Douglas, the reciting of the Gettysburg Address, Lee's surrender to Grant, a dream sequence in which Lincoln sees his own coffin lying in state inside the White House, and the assassination. The deathbed scene also is re-created. It is the earliest extant re-enactment of Lincoln's death.

Joe Henabery prays for guidance in D.W. Griffith's controversial classic, The Birth of a Nation *(1915).*

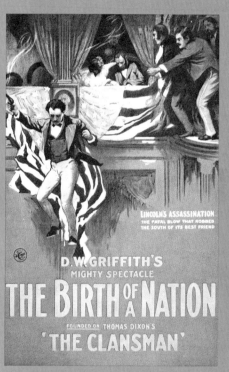

The president also appears in another 1915 film, *The Birth of a Nation*. D.W. Griffith's controversial epic was adapted from a book and a play by Thomas Dixon, a southern minister and white supremacist. The story revolved around the struggles of two families—one Southern, the other Northern—to survive the Civil War and Reconstruction. Dixon and Griffith shared a reverence for the martyred president, who was played by Joseph Henabery. Henabery, one of Griffith's extras, had twelve other roles in the film, as well! Tall and thin, Henabery applied his own makeup and putty nose after studying photographs of Lincoln in books borrowed from the Los Angeles Public Library. He exhibits great humility in the role. He appears sad-faced and stoop-shouldered, like he is carrying the entire weight of the nation on his back.

From a technical standpoint, the re-creation of the assassination in *The Birth of a Nation* is particularly interesting to watch. At the time, it was cinematography at its best. However, by today's standards, the film stock used by Griffith's cameraman was so primitive it looks to the modern viewer as if the scene had been photographed using one of Mathew Brady's Civil War cameras.

The shooting is followed by Booth's leap to the stage and his shouting of *"Sic semper tyrannis!"* While this is not the first filmed re-enactment of the assassination, it may well be the earliest dramatization of Booth's famous leap. The assassin was played by Raoul Walsh, who during filming sprained his ankle after landing on the stage. It would not be the last time an actor was injured re-creating this historic moment.

In 1924, Al and Ray Rockett spared no expense in producing *The Dramatic Life of Abraham Lincoln*, the first feature-length film to take the story of Lincoln back to his humble log-cabin beginnings. Unfortunately for film historians, no complete print exists. Surviving footage reveals how beautifully photographed, authentic-looking, and meticulously researched it was. The president was portrayed by George Billings, who wasn't an actor but who won the part because of his remarkable resemblance to the president. William Moran played a suave, debonair Booth, which did not sit well with the critics. ("Too attractive," declared *The New York Times*.)

Many Lincoln legends were dramatized for the first time in the Rocketts' silent film. These include young Lincoln trudging miles in the snow to return a book; fighting the town bully in New Salem; and, as the newly elected president, bidding farewell to friends and neighbors from the rear of a train at the Springfield depot. This emotional scene still exists, and it is wonderfully done. (One of the movie's reviewers was

Robert Sherwood, who went on to use it as the climactic scene in his Pulitzer Prize-winning 1939 play, *Abe Lincoln in Illinois*.) The Rocketts also chose to dramatize the story of Lincoln's love for Ann Rutledge. Previously, Lincoln's friend and law partner, William Herndon, had heard about the alleged romance, confirmed it through interviews with old-timers in New Salem, and included it in lectures and a popular biography. The love story (which many historians maintain never existed) had been dramatized only once before, in a 1914 Vitagraph picture called *Lincoln the Lover*.

Although he was a novice, Billings was quite convincing and enjoyable to watch. He gave Lincoln a more human dimension than previous actors

Although a bust at the box office, the 1924 silent film, The Dramatic Life of Abraham Lincoln, *perfectly recreated many scenes, including his death.*

had. In one of his most moving scenes, he holds a dying soldier in his arms inside a hospital, tears streaming down his cheeks. The assassination scene is accurately depicted, but the deathbed scene is truly remarkable. A room identical to the one in which Lincoln actually died was created especially for the film. Despite all the effort and money, *The Dramatic Life of Abraham Lincoln* was a box-office dud.

By 1930, silent films had been all but replaced by "talkies." D.W. Griffith devoted his first sound movie to his favorite president. It's difficult to understand why Griffith's *Abraham Lincoln*—which later was listed in the book, *The Fifty Worst Films of All Time*—received good reviews. It lacked the pace and grandeur of his earlier, silent works. The dialogue, supplied by Stephen Vincent Benet—who had won the Pulitzer Prize for *John Brown's Body*, a long narrative poem of the Civil War—was disappointingly wooden. So was the acting, with the notable exception of Walter Huston, who delivers one of the best-ever cinematic portrayals of the president. Huston deserved some kind of award just for getting through two pitiful scenes with Una Merkel, who was miscast as Ann Rutledge.

One of the most annoying features of Griffith's film is the license taken with Lincoln's legendary speeches. For example, one of his most famous statements—"A house divided against itself cannot stand"—was changed to "A house divided against itself must fall." History tells us that, upon being greeted by a cheering audience at Ford's Theater on April 14, 1865, Lincoln simply acknowledged the ovation and wordlessly took his seat. Griffith's Lincoln, however, is considerably more loquacious. In this scene, the president reminds the crowd of what he had said at his second inauguration a few weeks earlier: "With malice towards none, with charity for all," etc. For good measure, he then throws in the last sentence of the Gettysburg Address!

Griffith cast Ian Keith as Booth and in a barroom scene has the assassin cursing Lincoln for freeing the slaves. He then exclaims: "The man who kills Abraham Lincoln—will be an immortal!" Despite hamming it up, Keith's overall performance is marvelous. Twenty-eight years later, he was equally melodramatic as Booth's father in the Broadway play, *Edwin Booth*.

Lincoln (Frank McGlynn) and Booth (Francis McDonald) appear briefly in the 1936 film, *Prisoner of Shark Island*, directed by John Ford. It starred Warner Baxter as Dr. Samuel Mudd, imprisoned for having set Booth's fractured leg during his escape from Ford's Theater. In his only speaking scene, McGlynn stands in a White House window and asks the band to

Henry Fonda arrives in Springfield to start his career as a lawyer in John Ford's Young Mr. Lincoln *(1939).*

play "Dixie." Ford's treatment of the assassination is notable. In previous films, the movie audience is looking at Lincoln when he is shot. Moviegoers see his face contort and his head jerk—an image some reviewers had criticized as too graphic. Ford chose to merely show Lincoln's hand suddenly clench his *Our American Cousin* playbill for an agonizing second, before slowly fluttering to the ground.

Three years later, Lincoln was back on the screen in another Ford-directed film, this time in the person of Henry Fonda in *Young Mr. Lincoln*. The 1939 film tells two stories: Lincoln's love for Ann Rutledge and his successful defense of two boys accused of murder. The latter scenario was inspired by an actual case, in which Lincoln defended the son of his old friend, Jack Armstrong. The scenes between Fonda and Pauline Moore, who played Rutledge, are syrupy, but certainly an improvement over those between Walter Huston and Una Merkle a decade earlier. According to Lamar Trotti's script, Rutledge's death from a fever matured Lincoln and inspired him to greatness.

Young Mr. Lincoln is mostly unabashed fiction. Nonetheless, it is one of the most beautiful of all Lincoln films. The audience knows from the outset that this biopic is all about a man destined for greatness, so every scene is freighted with meaning. In the final scene, Lincoln walks to the top of a hill just as a storm begins. The audience understands that he's heading towards his destiny and a greater national storm that he will have to weather.

That same year Robert Sherwood's *Abe Lincoln in Illinois* was adapted for the screen. Raymond Massey reprised his stage role and Ruth Gordon co-starred as Mary Todd. The film shows Lincoln's moral and political development and illustrates some of his weaknesses, something never attempted before. However, whereas Henry Fonda's Lincoln was perceived as heading for a great destiny, Massey's Lincoln seems bound for tragedy. Although the real Lincoln was ambitious and very much his own man, the future president in *Abe Lincoln in Illinois* is controlled by outside forces. One of those forces is Mary Todd, pushing Lincoln for the sake of her own ambitions. *Abe Lincoln in Illinois* was the first play and film to dramatize her jealousy, possessiveness, and tenuous mental state. Sherwood's Lincoln is often a brooding, tragic figure, whose unstable wife's outbursts cause him great anguish and embarrassment and threaten his own sanity.

The climax is Lincoln's farewell speech as he leaves Springfield for Washington to pilot the nation in its darkest hour. The actual speech was short and to the point, but Sherwood cut out the middle passages and substituted his own words about dealing with the current crisis—a thinly veiled reference to the coming showdown between the forces of "good" and the fascist regimes of Germany, Italy, and Japan. This allegorical scene may have been the finest of Massey's career; certainly it was one of his favorites.

The 1955 feature, Prince of Players, *starred John Derek as John Wilkes Booth and Richard Burton as his brother, Edwin.*

Abe Lincoln in Illinois was an obvious choice for presentation on the fledgling postwar medium known as television. An early production starred Stephen Courtleigh, who had often been featured in the play's lengthy run; a 1950 television play starred Massey, cementing an already remarkably close public association with the role.

In 1952, the CBS-TV series *Omnibus* presented *James Agee's Lincoln*, an ambitious five-part drama inked by the talented screenwriter, poet, and film critic. Funding for the series came from the Ford Foundation. Agee was fascinated with the real and mythical sides of Lincoln and envisioned the series as more of a visual poem than a biography. Tall and lanky Royal Dano, who had been "the tattered soldier" in the screen adaptation of Stephen Crane's *Red Badge of Courage*, was Agee's own choice to play Lincoln. Dano's assets included a strong physical resemblance to his character and a midwestern twang.

Most of the episodes deal with the early formation of Lincoln's character. The restored village of New Salem was utilized extensively, except for interior scenes shot at a Manhattan studio. The Ann Rutledge romance is prominently featured (again), the role going to Joanne Woodward in her first television performance. Woodward's scenes with Dano are beautifully crafted and devoid of cluttered dialogue. For the first time, a Lincoln drama showcased Lincoln's mother, her tragic death, and the influence of his stepmother. This was all done as a flashback, as the first episode opened with Lincoln as president and moved quickly to his assassination. Agee was particularly fascinated with the issue of mortality, and his creative use of symbolism made this opening episode particularly effective. As one critic said, "It was a piece of pure film poetry."

The only drawback to the series was its sometimes slow pace. However, Agee's measured tread contributed to its finest moment: the scene showing Lincoln's body being transported back to Illinois for burial. As the steam-puffing train dutifully chugs along to its destination, Martin Gabel recites Walt Whitman's poem, "When Lilacs Last in the Dooryard Bloom'd." The pictures alternate between shots of the train passing wheat

fields, close-ups of the locomotive's headlight, and low-angle views of the
railroad ties whizzing past. Viewers get glimpses of the faces of the two

A scene from Prince of Players. *In an ironic bit of casting, Raymond Massey (left), famous for
his role as the president in the stage and screen versions of* Abe Lincoln in Illinois, *played
Booth's father.*

soldiers standing guard over the casket, grieving citizens lining the tracks,
a farmer plowing his fields who stops to respectfully remove his hat, and
an elderly black woman waving a handkerchief.

The first television play about Lincoln's assassin was *John Wilkes Booth*,
produced in 1949 and starring the handsome young John Baragrey.
Videotape was unknown in the early days of live television, and no
kinescope (a copy made from filming the image off a picture tube) is

known to exist, so little is known of this show except that it followed Booth through his escape to Virginia. In 1951, *The Spur*, an adaptation of the book by Ardyth Kennelly, appeared on *Philco Playhouse*. This time John Baragrey served as narrator while Alfred Ryder starred as Booth.

The Spur examined Booth's sanity and explored his motives in killing Lincoln. Two theories were presented, both of which have been soundly rejected by most modern historians. The first was that Booth had been losing his voice, due to improper training. The second was that Booth hated his more talented older brother and transferred his murderous feelings towards Lincoln. The program was perhaps poor history but did introduce a new element to film treatments of Booth. It was the first to go back to his childhood—specifically, a scene taken directly from his sister Asia's memoirs, in which a gypsy fortuneteller prophesied that the sixteen-year-old Booth would become rich and famous but would break many hearts and die a terrible death.

A 1955 feature film, *Prince of Players*, based ever so loosely on Eleanor Ruggles' 1953 book, dramatized the melancholy life of Booth's brother, Edwin. The death of his first wife and then the assassination weighed heavily upon his heart and mind but never diminished his brilliance as an actor. Edwin was played by Richard Burton, a good choice. John Derek was given the role of John Wilkes Booth. This, too, was excellent casting, for Derek looked more like Booth than anyone who has ever portrayed him. Unlike other "Booths," Derek did not have to jump to the stage from the box; a stuntman filled in. In an ironic twist, Booth's father was played by Raymond Massey, who for years had been strongly identified with his role as the president in *Abe Lincoln in Illinois*.

Prince of Players marked the first time the assassination was re-enacted in color—and in wide-screen Cinemascope, to boot. The film, like *The Spur*, takes the audience back to the assassin's early days on "the farm"—Tudor Hall in Bel Air, Maryland, which his father had started building before he died. There is very little fidelity to historical facts in *Prince of Players*. The senior Booth is seen bringing up his two boys and their sister, Asia, in a completed Tudor Hall, their mother having passed on. In truth, the father preceded the mother in death by many years, and there were four brothers and two sisters in the clan.

There also is a scene in which Booth is shot at the Garrett farm in Virginia. History tells us that just before he died, Booth muttered, "Tell mother I died for my country." However, since his mother had been killed off early by screenwriter Moss Hart, this celluloid assassin had to amend his final lines to "Tell *Asia* I died for my country."

Lincoln's last day has had particular appeal to dramatists. It was Jim Bishop, a popular syndicated newspaper columnist, who first mined its potential with his 1955 book, *The Day Lincoln Was Shot*. The factually flawed but best-selling volume traced Lincoln's and Booth's activities in Washington on April 14, 1865. Bishop's book was first dramatized on television in 1956 in a live color production on CBS. Raymond Massey returned as Lincoln in the only performance he ever gave as the president in which he was shot. Lillian Gish, although she looked nothing like Mrs. Lincoln (as was usually the case with actresses who portrayed her through the years), gave a fine performance. She was appropriately hysterical in the Petersen House, though some critics thought she had overdone it. (Incidentally, Gish had been in the audience in the assassination scene for *The Birth of a Nation* forty-one years earlier.)

Jack Lemmon, fresh from his role as Ensign Pulver in *Mister Roberts*, caught critics by surprise with his "surprisingly effective" performance as Booth in *The Day Lincoln Was Shot*. Lemmon played Booth as a vain, egotistical, and somewhat brooding character. Charles Laughton narrated, providing background, poetry, and chronology as the clock ticked away. The program shifted back and forth between Booth's and Lincoln's activities on that fateful Good Friday.

Lemmon was particularly effective in the three-minute monologue inside his hotel room as he prepared himself for the murder. He spoke to Lincoln in a mirror over his dresser, telling him that he, Booth, represented all of the South's victims crying out for retribution. Nobody in the national television audience knew that Lemmon was feeling some very real pain as he delivered his lines. During the afternoon dress rehearsal, he had ignored the advice of director Delbert Mann and attempted the twelve-foot leap from the box to the stage in order to get the feel of it. In making the jump, he sprained his ankle and had to be heavily taped for that evening's live performance. The camera shots had to be tightened so viewers watching in their living rooms could not see him limping *before* the assassination.

Other television productions to retrace Lincoln's movements on his final day were *Lincoln's Last Day*, a thirty-minute production by station WMAL in Washington, and *They've Killed the President!*, produced by David Wolper. Both programs were shot in 1968, but Wolper's did not air until 1972. They were inspired by the 1968 restoration of Ford's Theater, which provided the ideal setting for re-enacting the assassination.

Lincoln's Last Day was shot entirely in the cinéma vérité style, from Lincoln's and Booth's points of view. For the first time, actual relics of the

One never knows when or where Lincoln will pop up on the screen. Here he appears with Mr. Spock and Captain Kirk in a 1969 episode of Star Trek.

assassination, such as Booth's pistol, were used. The program ended at the original receiving vault in the Springfield cemetery where Lincoln was buried before being moved permanently to the Lincoln Tomb. Lincoln was never shown, though his shadow passed once across the screen. Booth was seen only in a slow-motion re-enactment of his leap to the stage.

Wolper's one-hour production told the story in modern documentary style, as shaken eyewitnesses were interviewed. Once again, Booth was not seen until he suddenly jumped from the box. Joseph Leisch, a nonactor, played Lincoln. He was depicted attending the afternoon cabinet meeting with General Grant and preparing to go to the theater with Mrs. Lincoln. All of the re-enactments were filmed in a warm sepia color, giving them an archival look. The assassination was "captured" on film as though a news crew had been on hand that night. Booth's leap was made by Robert Leonard, one of Wolper's production assistants. True to form, Leonard banged up his knee upon landing on the stage—the third "Booth" on record to have injured himself while re-tracing the assassin's famous exit.

One would think that by the time these programs appeared there would be nothing left about Lincoln to dramatize. Wolper proved that this was not the case. He purchased the dramatic rights to Carl Sandburg's Pulitzer Prize-winning Lincoln biography and produced a six-part television series, *Sandburg's Lincoln*, which aired in 1974. The half-dozen writers hired to write the six episodes utilized a wealth of untapped material to its maximum creative potential, with a minimum of historical license. Hal Holbrook, who journeyed to Kentucky and southern Illinois to study regional accents, was faithful in preparation, if not in looks, as Lincoln. Sada Thompson played Mary Todd Lincoln.

One episode concentrated solely on Lincoln's skillful use of humor to reduce personal and political tension. Another dramatized the awful commotion Mrs. Lincoln created when she publicly upbraided her husband for riding alongside a general's wife during a military inspection in the closing weeks of the war. The miniseries included a very tender scene in which the Lincolns embraced in grief over the death of their eleven-year-old son, Willie. *Sandburg's Lincoln* was the first film treatment of two women in Lincoln's life other than Mary Todd and Ann Rutledge: his aged step-mother, who had raised him, and Mary Owens, with whom he had an unsuccessful courtship.

Unfortunately, space does not permit a more comprehensive look at all of the movies and television programs devoted to Lincoln and his assassi-nation. The president has made cameo appearances in miniseries like *The Blue and the Gray* (Gregory Peck) and *North and South* (Hal Holbrook). Some programs, such as *The Perfect Tribute* (starring Jason Robards, Jr.), are completely fictional but contain wonderful acting. Others, such as *Vidal's Lincoln* (starring Sam Waterston and Mary Tyler Moore) and *Dream West* (with F. Murray Abraham as Lincoln), are forgettable. While the quality of the productions has been uneven, the genesis of these and future efforts remains consistent: an urge to dramatize one of the most fascinating episodes in American history.

Richard E. Sloan is a television engineer in New York. He is co-founder and past president of the Lincoln Group of New York and an authority on how Lincoln, Booth, and the assassination have been portrayed on film and stage.

For Further Reading

Stephen M. Archer. *Junius Brutus Booth: Theatrical Prometheus*. Carbondale: Southern Illinois University Press, 1992.

"The Assassination of President Lincoln." *Lincolnian* (March/April 1986).

Jean H. Baker. *Mary Todd Lincoln*. New York: W.W. Norton, 1987.

Roy P. Basler, et al. (eds.). *The Collected Works of Abraham Lincoln*. Springfield, IL.: Abraham Lincoln Association, 1953. 8 vols.

The Body in the Barn: The Controversy Over the Death of John Wilkes Booth. Clinton, MD.: The Surratt Society, 1993.

John C. Brennan. "John Wilkes Booth's Enigmatic Brother Joseph." *Maryland Historical Magazine* (Spring 1983).

George S. Bryan. *The Great American Myth*. New York: Carrick & Evans, 1940.

Helen Jones Campbell. *The Case for Mrs. Surratt*. New York: G.P. Putnam's Sons, 1943.

Francis B. Carpenter. *Six Months at the White House with Abraham Lincoln*. New York: Hurd & Houghton, 1866.

Samuel Carter III. *The Riddle of Dr. Mudd*. New York: G.P. Putnam's Sons, 1974.

Bruce Catton. *Never Call Retreat*. Garden City, NY: Doubleday, 1965.

Roy Chanlee. *Lincoln's Assassins*. Jefferson, NC: McFarland, 1990.

Salmon P. Chase. *Inside Lincoln's Cabinet*. Edited by David Donald. New York: Longmans, Green, 1954.

Asia Booth Clark. *John Wilkes Booth: A Sister's Memoir*. Edited by Terry Alford. Jackson: University of Mississippi Press, 1996.

Champ Clark. *The Assassination*. Alexandria, VA: Time-Life Books, 1987.

William H. Crook. "Lincoln's Last Day." *Harper's Monthly* (September 1907).

Richard N. Current. *The Lincoln Nobody Knows.* New York: McGraw-Hill, 1958.

David Miller DeWitt. *The Assassination of Abraham Lincoln and Its Expiation.* Freeport, NY: Books for Libraries Press, 1909.

David Herbert Donald. *Lincoln's Herndon.* New York: Alfred A. Knopf, 1948.

David Herbert Donald. *Lincoln.* New York: Random House, 1995.

Dorothy Fox. "Home of an American Arch Villain." *Civil War Times Illustrated* (March/April, 1990).

Richard B. Garrett. "End of a Manhunt." *American Heritage* (June 1966).

Timothy S. Good. *We Saw Lincoln Shot: One Hundred Eyewitness Accounts.* Jackson: University Press of Mississippi, 1995.

Ulysses S. Grant. *Personal Memoirs of U.S. Grant.* New York: Chas. L. Webster, 1885. 2 vols.

John A. Gray. "The Fate of the Lincoln Conspirators." *McClure's Magazine* (October 1911).

Charles Hamilton. *Lincoln in Photographs: An Album of Every Known Pose.* Norman: University of Oklahoma Press, 1963.

William Hanchett. *The Lincoln Murder Conspiracies.* Urbana: University of Illinois Press, 1983.

T.M. Harris. *Assassination of Lincoln.* Boston: American Citizen Co., 1892.

John Hay. "Life in the White House in the Time of Lincoln." *Century Magazine* (November, 1890).

Burton J. Hendrick. *Lincoln's War Cabinet.* Boston: Little, Brown, 1946.

Harold Holzer, Gabor S. Boritt, and Mark E. Neely, Jr. *The Lincoln Image: Abraham Lincoln and the Popular Print.* New York: Chas. Scribner's Sons, 1984.

John Gabriel Hunt (ed.). *The Essential Abraham Lincoln.* Avenel, NJ: Portland House, 1993.

Michael W. Kauffman. "John Wilkes Booth and the Murder of Abraham Lincoln." *Blue & Gray Magazine* (April 1990).

Michael W. Kauffman. "Booth's Escape Route: Lincoln's Assassin on the Run." *Blue & Gray Magazine* (June 1990).

Michael W. Kauffman (ed.). *Memoirs of a Lincoln Conspirator.* Bowie, MD: Heritage, 1996.

Richard M. Ketchum. "Faces from the Past: The Booths: John Wilkes, Edwin, and Junius." *American Heritage* (October 1961).

Stanley Kimmel. *The Mad Booths of Maryland.* New York: Dover, 1969.

Dorothy M. Kunhardt and Philip B. Kunhardt, Jr. *Mathew Brady and His World.* Alexandria, VA: Time-Life Books, 1977.

Dorothy M. Kunhardt and Philip B. Kunhardt, Jr. *Twenty Days.* New York: Harper & Row, 1965.

Philip B. Kunhardt, Jr., Philip B. Kunhardt III, and Peter W. Kunhardt. *Lincoln: An Illustrated Biography.* New York: Alfred A. Knopf, 1992.

Clara Laughlin. *The Death of Lincoln.* New York: Doubleday, 1909.

Margaret Leech. *Reveille in Washington.* New York: Harper & Row, 1941.

Lloyd Lewis. *Myths After Lincoln.* New York: Harcourt, Brace, 1929.

James Mackay. *Allan Pinkerton: The First Private Eye*. New York: John Wiley, 1997.

William S. McFeely. *Frederick Douglass*. New York: W.W. Norton, 1991.

James M. McPherson. *Battle Cry of Freedom*. New York: Oxford University Press, 1988.

Jacob Mogelever. *Death to Traitors: The Story of General LaFayette C. Baker, Lincoln's Forgotten Secret Service Chief*. Garden City, NY: Doubleday, 1960.

Mark E. Neely, Jr. *The Abraham Lincoln Encyclopedia*. New York: McGraw-Hill, 1982.

Stephen B. Oates. *To Purge This Land With Blood: A Biography of John Brown*. New York: Harper & Row, 1970.

Stephen B. Oates. *With Malice Toward None: The Life of Abraham Lincoln*. New York: Harper & Row, 1977.

Stephen B. Oates. *Abraham Lincoln: The Man Behind the Myths*. New York: Harper & Row, 1984.

George J. Olszewski. *Restoration of Ford's Theater*. Washington, D.C.: U.S. Government Printing Office, 1963.

Betty J. Ownsbey. *Alias "Paine": Lewis Thornton Powell, the Mystery Man of the Lincoln Conspiracy*. Jefferson, NC: McFarland, 1993.

Benn Pitman. *The Assassination of President Lincoln and the Trial of the Conspirators*. New York: Funk & Wagnalls, 1954.

Jane Polley (ed.). *American Folklore and Legend*. Pleasantville, NY: The Reader's Digest Association, 1978.

J.C. Power. *Abraham Lincoln — His Great Funeral Cortege from Washington City to Springfield, Illinois — With a History and Description of the National Lincoln Monument*. Springfield, IL.: J.C. Power, 1872.

James G. Randall. *Lincoln the President: Springfield to Gettysburg*. New York: Dodd, Mead, 1946. 2 vols.

James G. Randall. *Lincoln the Liberal Statesman*. New York: Dodd, Mead, 1947.

James G. Randall. *Lincoln the President: Midstream*. New York: Dodd, Mead, 1952.

James G. Randall and R. N. Current. "How Lincoln Would Have Rebuilt the Union." *American Heritage* (June 1955).

W. Emerson Reck. *A. Lincoln: His Last Twenty-four Hours*. Jefferson, NC: McFarland, 1987.

John Rhodehamel and Louise Taper (eds.). *"Right or Wrong, God Judge Me": The Writings of John Wilkes Booth*. Champaign: University of Illinois Press, 1997.

James A. Rhodes and Dean Jauchins. *The Trial of Mary Todd Lincoln*. Indianapolis: Bobbs-Merrill, 1959.

Eleanor Ruggles. *Prince of Players, Edwin Booth*. New York: W.W. Norton, 1953.

Gordon Samples. *Lust for Fame: The Stage Career of John Wilkes Booth*. Jefferson, NC: McFarland, 1982.

Carl Sandburg. *Abraham Lincoln: The Prairie Years*. New York: Harcourt, Brace, 1926. 2 vols.

Carl Sandburg. *Abraham Lincoln: The War Years*. New York: Harcourt, Brace, 1939. 4 vols.

Gene Smith. *American Gothic: The Story of America's Legendary Theatrical Family — Junius, Edwin, and John Wilkes Booth*. New York: Simon & Schuster, 1992.

Larry Starkey. *Wilkes Booth Came to Washington*. New York: Random House, 1974.

John Starr, Jr. *Lincoln's Last Day*. New York: Frederick A. Stoles, 1922.

Philip Van Doren Stern. *The Man Who Killed Lincoln*. New York: Literary Guild of America, 1939.

Smith Stimmel. *Personal Reminiscences of Abraham Lincoln*. Minneapolis: William H.M. Adams, 1928.

Charles B. Strozier. "Lincoln's Life Preserver." *American Heritage* (February 1982).

Charles Sabin Taft. *Abraham Lincoln's Last Hours*. Chicago: Blackcat Press, 1934.

John M. Taylor. *William Henry Seward: Lincoln's Right Hand*. New York: Harper Collins, 1991.

Tom Taylor. *Our American Cousin*. Washington, D.C.: Beacham, 1990.

Benjamin P. Thomas and Harold M. Hyman. *Stanton: The Life and Times of Lincoln's Secretary of War*. New York: Alfred A. Knopf, 1962.

William A. Tidwell. *April '65: Confederate Covert Action in the American Civil War*. Kent, Ohio: Kent State University Press, 1995.

William A. Tidwell, James O. Hall, and David W. Gaddy. *Come Retribution: The Confederate Secret Service and the Assassination of Lincoln*. Jackson: University Press of Mississippi, 1988.

Thomas Turner. *Beware the People Weeping: Public Opinion and the Assassination of Abraham Lincoln*. Baton Rouge: Louisiana State University Press, 1982.

Thomas Turner. *While Lincoln Lay Dying*. Philadelphia: Union League of Philadelphia, 1968.

Glyndon G. Van Deusen. *William Henry Seward*. New York: Oxford University Press, 1967.

Louis Weichmann. *A True History of the Assassination of Abraham Lincoln and of the Conspiracy of 1865*. New York: Alfred A. Knopf, 1975.

Elden C. Weckesser. *His Name Was Mudd: The Life of Dr. Samuel A. Mudd, Who Treated the Fleeing John Wilkes Booth*. Jefferson, NC: McFarland, 1991.

Francis Wilson. *John Wilkes Booth*. Boston: Houghton Mifflin, 1929.

Photography and Illustration Credits

AUTHOR'S COLLECTION: 109, 130, 131, 135, 159, 166, 169 (both), 183.

BOSTOM MUSEUM OF FINE ARTS: 118 (bottom).

BURTON HISTORICAL COLLECTION: 10–11, 13, 117 (all), 119 (top), 123 (both), 124 (bottom), 137.

CAPITOL HOUSE, Topeka, Kansas: 9.

CHICAGO HISTORICAL SOCIETY: 34, 92, 118 (top left).

CHICAGO TRIBUNE: 86.

EDISON INSTITUTE: 203.

GEORGETOWN UNIVERSITY LIBRARY: 144, 147.

GEORGIA STATE ARCHIVES: 52 (left).

HISTORIC SEWARD HOUSE: 87 (both), 89, 191.

ILLINOIS STATE UNIVERSITY: 8.

IMP/GEH STILL COLLECTION: 206.

MICHAEL W. KAUFFMAN: 40, 41, 42 (both), 43, 44, 45, 57, 65, 143, 149, 152, 192 (right), 194.

LIBRARY OF CONGRESS: x, 5, 6, 7, 16 (top), 19, 20, 22 (top), 23, 24, 26 (top two), 27, 29, 32, 38, 52 (right), 54, 59 (both), 61, 67, 68, 70, 72, 73, 82 (both), 98, 100, 101, 106, 114, 122 (all), 124 (top left), 160, 161, 170–71, 175, 218.

MONROE COUNTY HISTORICAL ASSOCIATION: 25.

NATIONAL ARCHIVES: 17, 14–15, 16 (bottom), 21, 22 (bottom), 26 (bottom), 104, 108, 118 (top right), 156.

NATIONAL GALLERY OF ART: 119 (bottom), 120 (bottom).

NATIONAL PARK SERVICE: 18, 79 (right), 83.

LLOYD OSTENDORF: ii, 2 (left), 4 (all), 50–51, 55, 91 (bottom), 121 (all), 124 (top right), 135, 188, 199.

BETTY OWNSBEY: 88, 177, 178, 180.

RICHARD E. SLOAN: vi, viii, xi (both), 2 (right), 76–77, 79 (left), 80, 85, 90 (both), 91 (top), 94–95, 96, 110 (both), 111, 113, 132–33, 140, 158 (both), 165, 190, 192 (left), 195, 196 (both), 202, 204 (both), 208, 210, 212, 215.

SURRATT SOCIETY: 163 (both).

WHITE HOUSE ASSOCIATION: 120 (top).